CHAPTERS

Vanessa Nocera

LAST CHANCE OF ESCAPE

It all started in 2003…

I remember waking up in the middle of the night.

I opened the bedroom door, reached the bathroom. I was distracted by my parent's voices. They were arguing about a short business trip that my Dad was planning to take, to save the flat from being forced into sale at auction.

He was a good-looking man, 6 feet tall, with brown hair and green eyes. A wise man, very polite all the time, and every person fell in love with his 'Posh attitude, He was passionate about making money and he could set up a dream business in a very short time.

He was smart and fast in concluding a deal.

He was that kind of guy who was good at selling, maybe I might say good at talking but I think the right word is lying. He would lie about everything; especially while he was working. A mixture of a lawyer and a criminal, showing the care of a president to his clients.

But he was in debt with the government. He never paid a bill in his life. He was driving a white Ferrari, bought in my mother's name. A very good guy: that was the description used by his clients. He was involved in the very important business of fashion clothes around Italy; this was what my Mum and I were led to believe. He did not share a lot with us about his business; a good father to me and always there for me whenever I needed him.

The very first time I got my period, he was the only one who knew about it.

Although he promised me that was just our private secret, he spread the news around the whole family.

The day after the news, he organized a party, just for me.

He had two shops in the city centre and whenever I was there, he would always be busy with the cash flow, invoices, payrolls to issue and delivery. I remember a couple of times seeing two guys asking for money which he refused to give. The outfit of these guys is stylish and composed but imposing and negative and the way they speak to him is as though they were ready to push him to the limit and beyond. While he is meeting with them, I put my hands into his desk drawer, but to my horror I find that the gun was no longer there. Dad was always struggling with investments and he had some businesses in Addis Ababa, and Ethiopia as well.

He decided to go away for four days, although my Mum was far from happy about that trip.

I stopped thinking about it, as I was quite excited at the prospect of spending the weekend with Dad to go fishing together on his return. Standing by the High School at 7.55 a.m. it is a raining; 13th January 2003.

My Dad is kneeling.

He holds my hand, kissing my little fingers... tears on his eyes,

— Have a good day at school, Vany! Your Dad loves you! Never forget it, please!

He hugged me so tight that day…

I was only a teenager, and I didn't pay that much attention to those words.

I reach the last step of the stairway. My heart stops for a moment. Then I think, it is like I had a feeling that he was running away from me; but I needed to reach the class, so I decided to forget about that negative feeling and I keep walking through the corridor.

That Monday morning was the last time I saw my Dad…

Late evening of a Friday it is raining outside, raindrops crashing against the window.

The house is empty, my Mum is setting up the table for 3.

I stop, and say:

— Mum, when Dad is coming back? Is it today? She gazes at me.

— Yes, Honey, it is tonight, not sure about the time.

Food is getting cold, she says.

Pasta is ready on the plates. We start eating and watch the News.

When we had a dinner with Dad, it was quite fun and lively; he was always talking about something, we never had a quiet dinner before.

Mom was much too quiet that night.

She was a pianist; she dedicated all her life studying Music.

We had a Piano in the living room and when the cat was walking on it, we could hear the notes from our bedrooms, but it was not really enjoyable to be woken up by disjointed piano sounds in the dark night hours.

Then you realize that is him.

Ambrogio, grey hair on the top of his body, green eyes, and white hair on his stomach and around his cheecks; he was a very big cat.

I was not really interested in learning how to play a piano, although Mum was trying to push me to do so. She stopped her dream job because she was helping Dad with the business.

I was 13 years old at that time experiencing all the new steps that a teenager discovers such as the first kiss or the first cigarette ; I used to write it all in my diary which I made sure was locked and I had the only key.

But still Dad knew everything about me, he was the only person that I ever felt very comfortable to talk to, he gave me good advice and never let me down.

So, I am asking to myself... Why has he left us? Why is he not here yet?

Does he maybe run away from something or someone?

It has been a week since he walked away from me that Monday at high school.

The police have been called by Mum. All the family are in the living room talking about my Dad missing. The cops arrive, start asking my Mum if he had any suspicious events or if she has seen anyone suspicious hanging around his business in the last week, she was aware about a short business trip and nothing more at all.

They also ask me if he was different with me during the last week; did he behave strangely or say anything odd. I didn't want to tell them about that the gun having disappeared from his drawer. So, I just looked at the policeman in the eyes and with a worried face, I say:

— No, I'm afraid, but I have not noticed anything strange during the last week.

— OK fine, if something comes to mind, please call us!

— Sure, I will...

I would tell the truth if the cops were genuine, but I did not like the way they looked at my Mum; they make me feel uneasy. I had a feeling that Dad was in trouble, as I remember those guys walking with him outside the shop, trying to ask for money.

I was not too sure if I need to say this to Mum, so I decided to keep it for myself.

It has been two weeks since my Dad left.

I heard my mum crying in the middle of the night; she was waiting for me to fall asleep, unaware that I too could not sleep.

I am feeling so weak from this, I don't know if I can handle it, is hard to ignore my Dad's unexplained absence.

Looking the stars of my bedroom wall... and thinking about him... Dad bought for me those Phosphorescent Stars that you can stick on the wall, so when the light was off, I could see the bright stars in the dark sky.

I'm feeling I am in an open space.

I try to have a silent cry, so I decide to push the pillow over my neck, then push with my palms against my head. I spent all the night crying, so that the next morning my eyes were swollen.

It is morning, and I am getting ready for school.

For my first time, I am walking to School as Dad always drops me off with his car.

I was looking for him in the street, by the entrance of the shops, in the School; I was always checking every corner to see where he could be.

I try to keep myself awake; yes, I am awake now, I thought it is just a dream that will end.

Like a nightmare that will stop once you open your eyes, but this time it was not a nightmare, it was not a dream... it was unwelcome reality.

It is windy, and the birds are welcoming me by the steps of my High School.

The road is empty, empty like my heart now, empty like the most beautiful vase without flowers, empty like the sky without stars, empty like a wedding without the bride.

I was feeling like a walking body without my organs, a cold sensation across my mind, crushing my souls.

I stop by the last step, ready to reach the entrance. I was locked in the space for a moment like you are divide from the world, far away from people, far away from the noise of the students, far away from the chatter of the parents; it is like you stop the clock and meditate for a moment.

That moment was my worst enemy, he didn't give me any notice when he came, he just came and destroyed the day, he destroyed my chat, he made me a loser, keeping my concentration far away when I try to study; I have been trying to control him but there was a strong negative energy against me, the energy of this enemy was too big for me to handle, I have to accept it is the biggest enemy in the world.

The depression, I have decided to give him a name, well, her name was Black Moon.

Everyone at school was aware about my Dad missing. The teacher suggests talking with a child therapist, but that would not be enough for me to discover the truth.

I have decided to start learning how be calm and keep myself in a positive mood.

I join the after school just to keep myself busy. This was not a good idea, as I saw other dads waiting by the entrance to pick up the kids; I was thinking about my Dad.

I have decided to join the Gym. In the middle of a class they are playing a song. It is the very song Dad was singing to me; I cannot hold back the tears. The teacher told me to take a break. In the changing room I imagine my Dad still talking with me, then the reality again, myself and an empty soul, crying in my own in the toilet of the gym-changing room.

Losing myself in the middle of the street, I saw the Church at the end of the road.

I walked in and started to cry. There is no time for happy moments; I only know I must let this feeling out.

Looking at Mary standing by the altar and asking where my Dad could be, I am praying about a call, just a call so I can hear his voice and feel better.

A Priest is walking towards me; he smiles and he asks if I need a confession.

— I don't know any more, I say. — If it helps my Dad to come back, maybe, I added.

— Hold my hand, he says, tell me what's wrong and what happened; you shouldn't stay by yourself in the Church.

— My Father has been missing and I am unable to continue with my life; I am feeling demotivated, I tell him.

He starts looking at me and he pause for a minute.

— Pray for the strength to come straight into your heart and deal with it, deal with negativity; God will give you the light, the Hope and the Strength to ensure you can continue your life with your Dad or without him. You are young and smart; you should enjoy the life of a teenager! If your Dad will not return, you have to be ready to let this negativity go away from your heart or it will destroy you; it will drag you down. I want you to pray every day and when you feel lost, the Church is always open for you and I am always here. I am Father Andrea, and I am very happy to see you here; this will be your secret place, very quiet, where you can cry, think and meditate in peace, without any distractions; no one will see your sadness or understand your madness. People are too busy to focus on your Dad missing. They only want to see what they want to see. But there is one person in your life that cares about you and love you so much. One person who is more special than your Dad and he will never run away from you. He can be your friend as well; people don't care very much about your case. But God... He will care about you!

For the first time, I begin to see the light; a sign of happiness is coming back in my heart.

That day was the beginning of my strength.

I was not feeling alone; I was finally calm.

The storm is going away, and I can see flowers around me.

Twice a week, I visited the church, helping the Priest with the cleaning, candles, and Mass.

He also offers me the chance to spread the words of the Bible around the area for about 10 euros a day.

That positive purpose and influence saves me from the depression.

It is one week until my birthday.

I have done my homework. I had some savings from the Bible advertising and now I am thinking more positively; although the atmosphere is heavy, I try to stay positive.

Mum is ready to talk with me about my Birthday.

— Honey, you will be 13 soon! What would you like to do?

— Mum, you know what I want? I want Dad here with us again, please...

She starts crying, telling me, I want it as well, love. I am sorry if I am not consistent with you as a Mother, she added, I am trying, but I am on my own as well!

— Mum... Is something that I really want to do for my birthday! I want to go to the Car Wash and stay inside the car while the car is being washed!

— That's all? She says.

— Yes Mum. Please, can we do it for my birthday?

— Come on Vany, we don't have to wait the birthday for that, we could maybe go this coming Friday! Then we will get some take away and go to the cinema! She looked at me.

— Mum, thank you very much, I respond excited!

My Birthday was on Saturday. I started to look to find the movie that I want to watch, and my friend Laura asked me what I want as a present.

Suddenly, after long time, I was quite happy that week, as I know I was surrounded by people who loved me.

It is Friday, and I am wearing my favourite jeans, a hoodie, and trainers. We arrived at the Car Wash and with a glass of Coke in my hand. I am ready to see the show!

The car gets up, seems like I am flying; soap starts to come over the windows, water around spread from every place of the machinery, while I am drinking the best part of it; is coming…

The sponges! Yes, the sponges time!

The brushes are cleaning the car up and down; it's like a mix of raining and snowing in between. 5 minutes of it and car is going on the ground floor; the air is coming.

My Mum is happy as I am enjoying the simplicity!

— Look at you! She says, You are so excited! A selfie come up straight away from her camera. Happy Birthday my Love! I am feeling grateful, she says. She looks at me drinking the Coke, so what movie shall we watch?

— I don't know. I'm still deciding between 8 Mile or Titanic. Titanic, I think. Mum, yes Titanic!

— Ok, look, I was thinking because you are doing very good at school you can watch Titanic tonight with me and 8 Mile next week. What do you think?

— Yes, Mum! Thanks I love you! I responded.

It is been 3 hours since the movie starts at, we still watching!

It was quite sad; the tears came naturally when Jack died! We have finished the movie and a pack of tissue to dry our tears!

We went to my favourite Chinese restaurant. We ordered some spring rolls and plunkings. Chicken fried rice as well and crab and lettuce soup, with a satisfied night we finish walking by the sea and look the stars above our heads.

It is Saturday. I receive a Birthday Cake from my school mates, a bag and a pen with my initials. I also invited my friends for an afternoon tea in my house as I know a part of my family will be there as well.

With cakes, candies, good company and pictures my Birthday is perfect and my mood is getting better, until my phone rings. I had a Nokia at the time. I was ready to get the phone next to me, when I was distracted by my friend playing with the balloons. I kept my phone in my pocket just in case it rings again...

1 missed call, unknown number; well, is a bit mysterious, as it is also my special day.

I am going to the bathroom, here it goes again; I feel the vibration in my jeans pocket and it is an unknown number again.

I answer pressing the green bottom, quiet I am listening without saying Hello.

— Vany? Baby? It's Dad!

My heart stopped, my hands were shaking...

— Dad? Where are you? Are you OK? I have been looking for you for 2 months!

— Vany! My love, my darling, I miss you so much. Happy Birthday! He added.

I start crying, cannot talk any more, tears did not give me the possibly to have a word out of my mouth.

He starts, Vany, remember that I love you so much, you do not need to cry. I will come back to you, I will come back soon, because I love you! Be strong, please!" I must go now! Be safe Vany. He hungs up the phone.

2 minutes of phone call, after 2 months that I am not talking to him!

Such a shame! I took a tissue from the bedroom.

I start crying too loud that my Mum and my grandparents came to the room.

They ask:

— Vanessa? Oh God! Love, we are here, what happened?

— Dad called few minutes ago, I say.

My Mum was disappointed to see me upset, as soon she saw me crying, she started crying as well.

— He called me for only 2 minutes, but with just those 120 seconds, he destroyed my whole week.

Everyone questioned me where was he, which number he called from.

No proof, no evidence, just Happy Birthday!

He did not mention where he was, just that he was coming soon.

We telephoned the police and informed them about the phone call.

My friends are in the living room.

I inform them that the Party is over as my dad just called.

Laura is the only one who persuaded me to continue to enjoy the evening.

With the piece of cake in my hands and sad eyes, I thanked everybody and shut the main door.

Helping my Mum with the cleaning, I am still upset. I still cannot believe about that call…

Six months later, another call, telling me that he is safe, and he missed me; he still did not mention when he is coming and where he is living; weird chatting and questions were flooding my mind…

From that time, I know when my father was calling me… occasionally, six times in a year, every phone call is about two minutes, no ID number, no locations.

Why? Is he maybe a dangerous person? Or he is in danger? Does he escape from someone?

I was almost there to know it.

Sicily and the Mafia

A beauty of an Island surrounded by prickly pears (fico d'India), hugged by the Blue of the Mediterranean Sea, capers-covered caves, the natural white beach across the perimeter of the land. Land of Love and Passion!

Yes, this island is very beautiful, every moment of my life I can remember the best of it; every positive moment spent there was important and full of meaning. You can find real men there; the one who is vital, jealous, authoritarian, passionate about socialising and awesome.

In Sicily anything and everything is possible. One day you could choose to be a dentist, or a Beautician, a teacher, or to maybe open your very own business. As long you have a connection and you know the right people anything is possible this is because a good helping-hand recommendation or bribery and corruption is a very popular Made in Italy product! And in Sicily is worse than the rest of Italy!

For most jobs, when you attend for an interview they ask for too many skills but the reality is that you might not be the right candidate for them, not because you are not clever enough but maybe you are not the daughter of a particular Doctor, you are not the cousin of the President, you are not the son of the Minister. So if you are not well connected, they don't want to say the true reason to you and instead they point to your CV telling you they need someone who speak German or Russian or they prefer someone who has a pilot's licence or aircraft training; for sure they will always find an excuse for reject you or hire you! Therefore, I decide to escape from Sicily by joining the Air Force, but I knew that even there was like this too; when you think, it will be an organisation of total honesty and integrity, part of the reputation of the Government, unfortunately that feeling of perfect morality was only in my dreams.

I was only 13 years old when I first became involved with the Mafia. You get that certain respect from people when you walk around like you are important. Unfortunately, this is only what people see from outside, the first impression, but what do we really know of what is there behind that image? I was the first girl in the High School to drive a scooter at my age. I was driving a scooter every day to go to school; sometimes I would pick up my best friend, Laura who lived on the other side of the street. That scooter was called a Vespa Piaggio. It was illegal as it was modified from being 50 cc to about 125 cc. So, I easily remember how I used to enjoy the rush of speed of the fresh air during the Summer; that scooter, was everything to me. My family was disappointed when Grandad bought it for me as they were worried about the possibility that I could crash and put my life at risk.

I did not care at all about the risk, because the fantastic adrenaline was enough to make me fell alive, without that, I could fall back into my Black moon again.

I was driving with Laura one day by the seaside. A guy was having a spring bath totally naked. Laura and I were admiring his impressive body. I was driving and so I didn't notice the broken road in front me as I was distracted. I crashed the scooter and punctured both wheels. We had to walk for about 2 hours until we reached the first tyre repair shop.

Lucky that day I was with her as she lent me some money for the repair. Laura was very close to me; she never let me down. Her personality was quite strong, and she totally disapproved that I was involved in the Mafia. Because she cared about me so much, I decided to tell her everything that I was going through and all of my weakness.

Laura never judged me, she was there for me and she helped me as she was very good in keeping a secret; she was a loyal, clever girl, with huge green eyes, black curly hair and very calm attitude.

It has been a year since my Dad left Sicily. It has been a year that I am looking after his deals. The scooter was a good excuse to be independent and reach my friends, do what I needed to do and get home without arousing attention. Although we had a good Lawyer for our case, Dad did not send my Mum any money, so I decided to work.

My Mom did not know about it. She was struggling financially, so she decided to sell her car, a Fiat Panda; that car had given rides to everyone, it was quite small but very efficient. One day a storm damaged the seaside of the city of Siracusa, That day my Mum and I were driving home, crossing the road in a state of anxiety and panic that the car might break down at any moment; this did not happen as the car continued okay until we got safely home.

Although she sold the car, I did not want to use her money for schoolbooks and the admission fee, so I decided to start working at a Café in the local area. This cafeteria was opposite to a church. The business was managed by a cop, Stefano. He was a sexy cop, very fit; he worked out every day in the Gym; maybe that was the reason why I wanted the job so badly. He had brown hair and black eyes, nice cheeks when he smiled: his arms were massive and dark, his skin colour was gold, a mix between a good tan and his natural skin. He was a regular customer in the tanning shop as his girlfriend worked there, When he interviewed me, I told him I was 16 years old and I want to work because I love to be independent. He was training me every day, how to pour a drink, how to make an espresso, how to use the cash points; in one week I was ready to go.

He used to pay my wages as 'cash in hand' as he was aware of my school hours. The job was easy to do, flexible hours, although the money were not worth the time as I was
starting at 2pm and finish around 8pm. I used to earn about 20 euro daily, but I could not complain as I was getting enough salary for what I had planned. My daily routine was going to School and do the homework at School in the lunch break or any break available. I always tried to use the opportunity to review my essay with my brightest schoolmates, those who were more clever; I always got help from them and sometime we used their house or mine to review exams and in exchange I gave my scooter for a day during the week or I let them drive it with me.

My mother was working as a Home Help at that time, so she never really knew when I got home. She left for work around 13:00 and that was the time I finished school, go home refresh myself and run off to work. When I got home, I began to get dinner ready for her and help her with the housework. She usually finished around 9pm. Everything was running as usual until one day...

I had not noticed that my Mother was starting follow me. She was looking after me as usual, and our relationship was as normal as every day, but that day was different...

That day I was a bit tired with my school project, so I didn't have the time to stop home as usual instead I decided to take the scooter and drive to work. I started my shift as usual with the same people around; the regulars, those who start to drink first whisky at 2pm, and talking about the weather. I already knew who a new customer was and who was more special. Stefano was at the cash point busy with his staff. Everything was as usual, until I saw my mother!

As soon as she walked into the café, my heart stopped, my cheeks were red and my voice very shy.... I was thinking to use the toilet. To hide myself! But I did not want any trouble with the Boss. I decided to remain calm and see what Mum wanted and why she was there. She came with a friend to the Bar; she was not there for a coffee or a drink, She was there for me ...She opened the door and with a loud angry voice said:

— I knew it! I knew you were here! Why you lie to me? What is wrong with you? Are you a homeless person, that you need to work in this dirty Café, surrounded by old men ready for a chance with you? It is inadequate for you! Get out now!

I was listening to her and I tried to tell her that she was wrong as the Boss behaved well with me. As soon she looked into my eyes, I said:

— Mum, please I must pay the Admission fee for the school and I also need new clothes for September! I cannot leave now! I just started my shift!
She gazed at my boss, then she added:
— Excuse me Sir, do you know my daughter's age?
He says….
— Well, I know she is 16 years old, but she is very committed to her role.
— Really? My mother said…
— I am afraid she is only 13 and it is Illegal to hire a teenager without a contract!
— Well, my name is Stefano, I am a police officer, I am sorry that you react like that, but your
daughter told me she was 16, I am sorry for any inconvenience.
She looked him and took me with her, saying to Stefano:
— We are leaving! Goodbye!
— Vani! Why?
— This place is not for you! Let's go home!
— Let me be a Mother for you! I am really working hard to raise you properly; I am trying very hard trust me! Since your Dad left everything is on me! But you need to give me an opportunity instead of judging me all the time!

— Mum, I want to work and being independent please, I responded.

— Vany, you are a baby girl and this world is too dangerous for you! You are my baby girl and I cannot put you at risk! She continues to say…

— If you really want to work part time, I know an Ice cream place that would be suitable for you, then you will not serve whisky but ice creams.

That was true, that place was smelly and dirty as well,

— Yes Mum! I want to have a chat with the Owner of that ice cream place please, I said. I want to have a job! It was good to have cash in my purse every day!

Although she was not aware about the deals that I was taking with my Father's friends and that the work was also an excuse to continue my business.

I did not want to look too suspicious in my mother's eyes, to justify a lot of cash especially at my age was not easy. I need to work so at least I can tell her that the Boss decides to give me a pay rise or bonus or something similar. I did have a secure secret place where I was hiding my cash and the drugs, but she was the kind of Mother that she could find the impossible as she was good at finding everything!

My only big worry was I was scared she would find the Cocaine! But I had a solution for that as well. It is easy to confuse it with baking powder. So, I decided to empty some containers of baking powder and replaced the White! For the cash, well that was not difficult as I was working, however I did have a Barbie Doll. Yes, a Barbie, I used to cut the silk of her dress with a scissors, insert the cash, then fix it by sewing again. My Grandmother taught me how to sew. The first time that I sewed she put an orange on my hands told me to use it as a base, in order to help my finger passing the line with the needle. She also used to put money next to the orange if I start to sew with her. By the end of the year, all my dolls were transformed. I was very proud, and my family were aware how protective I was with my new decorated toys! They knew, that before touching any of them, they must ask me for my permission. Everything was quite manageable apart from the guns. It was far more difficult to hide the guns! Particularly because I did not want to separate them from the bullets, but I had to take the difficult decision to involve Laura in this. She knew about the guns and her family's garage at the seaside which was never used by her parents and was the best place for us. The first time she showed me the garage, I drove my scooter up to the door. Then I was carrying a lot of heavy metal; the bullets fell on the garage floor and when she saw them, she was a bit scared. But now we took every possible precaution and it was her idea to install a camera by the main entrance; so, we decided to get one! Sometimes, we used to go there and check the guns. One day we were drinking few beers and we started to practice shooting. She had learned shooting on empty dogfood tins and with all the practice we both became pretty good marksmen. We were quite ready to shoot a person but we did not want to go to prison, as a few of our friends were already there for too long and so we promised each other to always be good girls, find good husbands, raise a nice family, be good friends and good mothers.

I was walking to school, it was springtime. The flowers were in full bloom and the grass was very new with a fantastic smell of newness. The street was busy with cars stopped by traffic lights. My bag was full of books and I was totally ready to get an A pass mark for my essay because I had been studying very hard all the previous week.

Today I have the feeling that it will be a good day....

When, suddenly, two guys started walking close behind me. They were following my steps, walking in my shadow, breathing my perfume. I started to walk faster but they kept following me.bMy legs were shaking, and my heartbeat was racing. I stopped in the silence of the road. I turned around and I look them in the eyes! I recognised them; I saw them having a meeting with my Dad before he ran away! Of course, I remember they look so dodgy. I did not have a time to ask them what they wanted from me before a car stopped next to us and they push me inside the car. Nobody saw what happened to me in those 30 seconds; crazy that just half a minute changed my whole life. Although the road was busy, people walking to and from the store, the nearby petrol station full of customers queuing, and the post office already open. How come nobody saw it? How come nobody cared?

Or maybe they knew about those guys and they preferred to pretend not to see and decided not to call the police?

Or maybe they only saw what they wanted to see; this was the first time I learned about the Mafia. The three rules of it: do not talk about it, do not listen about it, do not see, and share it! On my own, with my school bag, 13 years old; my head started to feel that scary feeling of metal touching near my right ear. It is a gun! wait...!

I know that gun, that was my father's gun Berretta .92, how can I be scared of that gun; it was too familiar to me? I kept myself calm and relaxed and thought to find out why they came to me? Is my Dad alive or is living elsewhere? I think to myself.

They took me with them in the car! I did not cry or act as a babe because I wanted to discover the truth! But make no mistake, this was a proper Kidnapping!

In the car they told me that if I am quiet, it would not been necessary to drug me; therefore I was quiet and listened to what they were saying. They took me to the seaside. From the edge of the road, I saw a Villa. We parked outside, then, one of the guys pressed the buzzer. The wall was white and blue, with a palm tree outside by the car parking. At the gate, a German Shepherd dog barked viciously when we walked through the main entrance. A guy took my attention as he smoked a cigarette and held a gun in his right hand; he had a rosary around his neck, a scar on his left cheek, Of course, I was scared but I was very curious too. Also, I don't want to die here with these miserable boys. I was confused.

They took me into the living room of the Villa, passing by a jacuzzi located next to the swimming pool. The Villa is very nice but I'm not there to admire the place or the view. I continued to wait in the Living room; a lady asked me if I would like something to drink:

— Yes please, I said,

— Can I have a Sprite please?

— On the way to you, she responded.

It is only half nine in the morning and the living room is full of glasses and whisky ready to be served, to be served for who? I notice Luxury everywhere. Then I heard steps walking towards the sofa where I was sitting; a man came to me... A great man in his forties. He was wearing a suit, touching his tie with his fingers, he came to me and touched my face, then he said:

— Just like your father, beautiful and smart, how old are you now Vanessa?

— 13, I am 13, and I am too young for you, I added.

— I am Giuseppe, but you can call me Toto or better Padrino Toto, (Padrino stands for Godfather!)

I still think over, who is this guy?

What does he want from me?

I started to drink a bit of Sprite left over, and He asked me:

— How is school now? I heard that you are the best in the class!

— Well, I am very confident about you and your strength, you were always clever my daughter!

— My Daughter? I am not your daughter I responded

— Where is my father?

— Why have you given him all this stress? I said

— What do you want from him? What do you want from me?

— Vanessa, my darling, your Dad is good guy, he just needs a break from his life; sometimes, a man needs time for himself to think, he just need to take some space, nothing much. Don't you worry about your father, he is proud of you and I will make sure that you will be a respected girl in Sicily. I will make sure that nobody will touch you, because they have to first go through me in order to get to you. I don't like to waste your time as I know you are very busy teenager but I need a favour just a favour from you as you have the scooter and the Police never stop Angel faces like yours, he says.

— What favour?

— I need you to use your scooter to transport a present for me, just because I am your father's friend! I would offer you 500 euro every week if you promised to work for me and do the job properly! But there is one condition: No police involved, no friend involved, just you and I, he says.

I paused, I gaze him, what happens if I refuse it?

— Why would you refuse 500 euros per week? I think with that money you could support your

mum and stay comfortable. You are clever girl and I need someone like you, someone who

could be a leader in a team, someone around me who I can trust.

—Yes, Toto, I say, but I want to think about all you have said. It is tricky work and I need to be

sure before I take it, I responded.

He took me to school himself. He touched my knees and said, ok Vanessa, don't forget to open your bag after, there is a present for you!

I closed the car door and shook hands with him.

I was back in the school. I spoke with the teacher and told her that my Lawyer had something important to tell my mother and I, and that's why I couldn't make it to school in time. I know, teacher, I missed my exam! Is there anything that I can do in order to make it better now, please, I am begging you, She says — look Vanessa only for this time!

Grab a chair and start your assessment at the end of the tables by the corner.

— Oh, thank you so much I responded.
I finished my essay and used the lunch break to go to the Gym changing room to look inside the bag. 1.000,00 euros and a card saying, it was lovely meeting you today Vanessa, I hope we can work together, it is not just for me, do it for your Dad as well, as he loves you! I called Laura and told her to meet me at the changing room now. She came; I showed her the card and the money I took out a lighter and burned the card, then hide the money in my diary.

That is how my Gang Life started.

The bad things about drugs

I lost a lot of friends because they couldn't control this powerful drug. Cocaine. I saw people selling gold, houses, cars and in the most uncomfortable situations, even prostitution. Selling your body for this drug; isn't that cool? No, it is not. Because for the vulnerable, this drug will make them do anything. If you snort, smoke or inject cocaine or care about someone who does, you more than likely have some unanswered questions about the nature and effects of this powerful chem. Cocaine is a powerfully addictive stimulant that causes dramatic changes in the brain and behaviour. Common rich people used cocaine every day. Giuseppe asked me a favour. Which I didn't do for him, but in order to see my Dad again; I decided to collaborate with him. I used my scooter to become a drug dealer. The scooter I was driving was a black 50 CC Scarabeo Piaggio. The space reserved for the helmet was always full of cocaine. I stopped to work at the Bar because of the income when selling this drug was fast and double than the main salary. Every weekend I used to spend the night at the club. Different owners have been calling me to sell cocaine and doing delivery. Until one day, when I was driving from the club to a bar. The road is quiet, the moon is white and big and you can see its light on the sea. I cross the bridge; the air is fresh, and I am wearing a dress, a hoodie over my dress just to feel comfortable; I reached the edge of the bridge. Check point on the left and side. Police with dogs. I saw a police officer stepping his right foot and pulling out the stop point to me. Is waving and when I start to decelerate, my heartbeats stopped. For a moment I feel my teeth shaking up and down like when you get a high temperature. I start to smile at the police. He looks very serious and strict.

— Good evening, driving licence and scooter insurance.

— Yes Sir, here you are. How are you?

He didn't answer me.

He noticed a pack of Malboro Light on my upfront scooter space near the window.

— You are only 14 from your ID,14 years old; don't you think you are too young to smoke?

I am thinking about a smart answer... I gaze at him.

— Sorry sir, I have an exam next week at school and I am getting nervous as the teacher is very strict with the class and I want to score A+ on it, so sometimes I smoke, I know I am too young. I think I will give up now. You are right, I am too young to smoke.

— I hope so. Have a good night and drive safe! I turned on the scooter and I start driving till the edge of the Piazza.

I stopped for few minutes and just thinking about how much I was lucky. I started having adrenaline for few seconds, then I was calm again. I continue my journey, leaving the drug to the other club. Waiting to get paid. The envelope is coming, I am going to the toilet and checking the Cash. 2.000 Euros and a "thank you" card as I was on time. I start going outside the toilet and walking to the bar. A young guy is waiving at me; he called me by name and then he kissed my hand. He stopped me saying:

— Hey, you don't go nowhere, you stay here with me, Vanessa.

That guy was my neighbour; classic guy who was living the dream, growing up in a rich family; he was planning to study in Cambridge when he would be 18 years old.

Not a simple guy at all, very Posh all the time and sophisti-cated. He insists in offering me a drink and of course, I ac-cept. He is not by himself there but there are few girls around him ready for a line. His name was Patrik and he always offers Cocaine at the parties. I don't care about be-ing drugged with it, so he offers me a pill called MD; com-mon word is Ecstasy. I didn't take that pill, but his friend beg me for it so I decided to get rid of it giving the pills on his palms. I saw him dancing in a weird way and shaking his hands, sweating all over and acting like a crazy guy, then finishing wearing sunglasses at the party. The music is not good; techno music, so without being noticed from the guys, I walk away. I'm still thinking about that guy begging me for some Ecstasy, then acting different from his com-mon behaviour. Unbelievable. Cocaine, it is always there at every party waiting for us, ready to be snorted. But what we really know about Cocaine? Crack cocaine is derived from cocaine hydrochloride by taking powder cocaine, adding ammonia, or baking soda and heat to remove the hy-drochloride, and changing the ph. From an acid to its base alkaline form. This process makes the drug combustible, so it can be easily smoked. The resulting product is then broken into small pieces, or rocks, that can fit into a small pipe, or that can be packed into a cigarette or cigar. When crack is smoked, it is quickly absorbed into the blood through the lungs. It takes less than five seconds for the entire dose to reach the pleasure centre. For veteran users, just seeing the crack pipe approaching their lips accelerates this process, due to their learned anticipation of the cocaine effect. Because cocaine reaches the brain so rapidly, and before it reaches the liver, the enzymes designed to protect the brain and body from toxins like cocaine, cannot do so. The resulting "high" is immediate, intense, very compelling and addictive. When a drug is smoked, the psychoactive effects, addiction potential and harmful consequences are greatly increased. I saw people using cocaine in different ways: Chewing, snorting, injecting, and inhaling. Snorting is the most common way to use cocaine. I saw some of my good friends being addicted into it and they dissolved cocaine powder, combining it with heroin, and inject it. Many times I saw them on their journey, before, in the middle and after; it's like they are dreaming but they are there with you, watching movies or smoking a cigarette, when you are looking into their eyes you will understand that this drug will give you the worst sensations. I never forgot that guy's eyes; they looked like dead, like when you go to the fish market and you are buying those fishes; in order to buy the fresh one, you have to firstly check on the fish eyes. Dead like you don't have light on it, dead like you are in deep depression with your life, dead like you will never smile again. I never tried that Drug because I lost a lot of friends, so why should I? The "high" from cocaine is determined by the volume of the drug and by the speed at which it arrives at its targets in the brain. My friends described a cocaine euphoria that peaks in 10 to 20 minutes.

So how do I know if a friend of mine is using cocaine? The first thing I have to notice is a runny nose or frequent sniffles, dilated pupils, very black that if you see a girl with a blue eyes doing cocaine you will be very lucky to see her blue eyes as the black pupils are so dilated that you will not see the colour of the eyes. Another factor could be a long period of wakefulness followed by loss of appetite and over-confidence. You can feel so powerful in that hour that you could be a CEO for 60 minutes. This drug gives you too much over-excitement on the day that you use but on next day everything will change into a dark tunnel giving you paranoia, legal issues, missing or being late to work, financial problems, swing moods, and irritability depression.

Exstortion and the escape plan

One of the best investors would say that any economic crisis will affect his investments.

One of the best extortionists would say that the only concern in the business of extortion is the Euro; yes, the change to the Euro in the European Countries.

The Lira was the old currency in Sicily before the Euro was introduced in 2002.

Many people were struggling, businesses falling, big losses for the agricultural industry and when the country is falling, people survive only if they ask for money from the Mafia; not because they want to ask money from such horrible people, but because they have no choice; because they have children to feed; they are desperate, with no job, no money and a family to provide for.

So as soon as you are desperate, those people are ready to be your friends, helping at the same point, then waiting for the opportunity to act like the best moneylenders.

Suddenly, they give you a deadline.

The common sentences used for this was:

— I'll give you 48 hours to find the money! Or I will take half of your land! Then your wife, then give your bones to my pitbull's!

Unfortunately, those words were true.

And I was there, next to that family when I had to shoot that guy in his ankle.

I saw the blood gushing out of his muscles.

And someone told me after:

— Vanessa, you are too soft, but you will improve, it will take time. You are smart!

After that episode, nightmares are my best company when I sleep and nausea wakes me up in the middle of the night, thinking about that guy.

I was involved, too involved. I could not come back.

Sometimes I think if I came back to that day…

Yes, that day in my Father's business; talking to those guys, and let my mum know about those dodgy guys, that the gun was missing.

I kept my mouth shut, shut as now, that I was forced to kill someone who look like an honest guy, innocent, with a wife and a child.

I thank that moment when the bullet damaged his leg, instead of his heart.

However, they are still hurting him, just for a few thousand Euros.

This is the value of a person.

Then the Robbery paperwork.

Everyone was already waiting for that land. The extortionists were ready to make their profit, then me by the car, seeing the wife and the child crying from the window, praying God for his recovery, the moonlight and cigarette smoke over my skin.

The dog barked, the air was chilling and my reward was in the car.

Reward for being quiet, keeping everything inside my deep belly; I was dying to talk, I couldn't talk about it; they could kill my Mum and my Grandparents, I cannot think for a good plan at that moment, I have to finish school first.

The best solution will be to escape, not as the last time; escape in a different way, maybe joining the FBI, working for the Military Police, DNI...

One thousand Euros for being quiet and don't talk to anybody, waiting for me there, as soon as I touched that money, I was thinking what the word means when you call it dirty money, because to get that quick income, you did something dirty,

Then you heard that chilling chat, those people chatting about where should stop for an ice cream and petrol; then you think, why are those people talking about ice cream?

How can they even think about ice cream after killing somebody?

That day, one part of my brain was damaged.

I felt a part of myself was missing.

For those guys it is like a normal day at work, 9am until 5pm, but instead of taking the tube you are taking the bike or the car, instead of having an oyster they have a gun, instead of having gums, they have knifes, instead of having laptops, they have firearms.

Another common case of extortion came a week later.

I was in a villa, a villa by the sea, in the steam room inside a sauna.

A very big villa, massive, hard to visit all in one day.

I was in the SPA area when the temperature of the Sauna reached 180 degrees and they closed the entrance.

The guy was inside with his wife.

In every team there is a new entry; who was new in the group, was in charge to clean all the evidence.

Few weeks later that couple, were on the Missing People list.

A month later, I had my friend's birthday party in that villa! Six months later the villa had been sold; the buyer, of course, was Giuseppe.

The Godfather Giuseppe.

I was dying to talk to Laura about that.

Then, I stopped and think about her health; I didn't want her sleep to turn into nightmares, and so I kept it for myself.

I never lie, only if I need too.

One day, a random guy forced my house door trying to get into the kitchen to steal the TV, because inside the screen of the TV we used to keep cameras; those camera were connected to Giuseppe's TV, so if I get in trouble he could come or send somebody to help me.

That guy is also taking my dolls with him until when... Giuseppe saw him run away from my house...

Who was that guy? How did he know about my mystery dolls?

It was a friend of Laura, but Laura never said a word.

I know her personality and the way she is.

I was wrong.

That guy was sent by her, but why?

She wants me to stop with this life.

I cannot think about Laura now; I must plan something different and she was my best friend. I cannot hurt my best friend.

I was thinking... how can she do that?

Then, I stopped, and saw Giuseppe run away from my house telling me to jump on the back seat.

— On the back seat , right now?

— Yes, come on, we have not got much time! He added

I did it, of course,

Although I saw that guy, I didn't want to tell it to Giuseppe; I am sure he will kill him.

I didn't have time, unfortunately.

He followed that guy and crushed him with that motorbike, then leaving the street. Then getting back to crush him again and again, over his bloody skin with his wheel!

— I told you…. you need to tell me everything, you cannot hide anything to me. Nobody needs to mess up with my daughter! Go home now, try to rest as you had this trauma with this stupid guy! I am sorry about that Vanessa!

Sorry? I think.

You get rid of that guy like he was toilet paper, then you are sorry… I kept this thought to myself, then walked towards my house.

Unfortunately, when that guy tried to get into my house and forced the door, Giuseppe was around the house, otherwise things could have gone in a different way.

The most common feeling that I get is feeling guilty.

He saw that I was upset with him.

He is calling me; my phone is ringing…

— Hello?

— Vanessa, Giuseppe says. I didn't want this guy as the witness of something, please understand, he added. Remember this… It must be done! That guy cannot stay around like this, he will put you at risk, Vanessa. Is like a virus, he will spread the virus! You will go to prison and then I must visit you every day and I don't want this for you, you are a good girl, you are also going to school. Prison is not your future, my love, Your Dad will not be happy about it!

I did not know why he was so protective to me. I had a mix between hate and love with him.

He makes me feel uncomfortable sometimes, but he never touched me in a bad way; he always respected me, and he loved me in a good way.

He met my mother once, as he came during my assessment, then telling my mother that I am very clever, and I have done a fantastic presentation.

I was quite happy to see him.

He was there for me, teaching me how to drive a car, how to shoot, how to eat lobster, how to drink champagne when you are holding the glass.

Teaching me how to check for fake banknotes, how to handcuff a person and how to play pool.

Many days after school, we used to have meetings.

Our meeting was short, just a few minutes for a coffee.

Then, when he bought that villa by the sea, at my friend's birthday, he gave me a present.

A pool table in his living room.

He was teaching me how to play, then he gave the opportunity to enter the Regional competition with other people; he came with me during that competition.

I know it is not right to say that, but the guy for me was my Dad.

I used to have dreams about him, not nightmare, but hot dreams.

He was there for me anytime I wanted.

On Christmas time, he took me to the Cars Expo.

Then with his firm voice, telling me...

— Choose a car, a beautiful car for a beautiful woman.

I was seeing the white Fiat 500.

Then a smile came spontaneously staying on my cheeks...

— Drive it! Go for a quick ride! Drive around and see if you enjoy.

When I came back:

— How was it? Do you like the car?

— Of course, I added.

After a few minutes, he spoke with the supervisor guy and gave some tips.

The owner handed me the car keys.

When those keys touched the skin of my palm, I had goose bumps!

I drove around the city with the most popular car; my friends used to invite me to go to the cinema and go for a walk because they were in love with my car.

At that time, I realised who was the real friend, who was the fake one.

I saw Laura a few times at the cinema and at the shop.

Our friendship was changing...

I knew Laura's plan. So, I decided to use one of those fake friends to check something for me.

Since the time when that guy tried to force my house door, I never visited the garage where the guns were hidden.

I always had a feeling that in that garage something was waiting from me.

That guy was quite fast, he was a marathon runner and with his legs ran a lot of competitions around the country; he was quite popular.

So, I decided to offer him to drive my car only if he could check the inside area of the Garage for me, so I did.

I took him there, it was a bit late, but the light was still out, during sunset time,

I stopped the car.

In the silence of the forest you can hear only the motor of the car that was off still running and making some noise.

I looked into his eyes and said:

— Are you exited to drive my car? I will take some picture of you while you are driving.

He gazes at me, then says:

— Vanessa, finally I met you! You are very nice girl! Ok, now I am going… he added.

He starts to walk into the garage.

He walked for about four minutes to reach the garage door.

I lost sight of him; he must be by the door, I think.

He starts calling me.

— Hello?

— Vanessa, I am here by the door!

— Good! I say

— Please open the door.

— I cannot open it, is seems to be blocked by something from inside. Can you try to push it?

He tried to force that door with a key that he has in his pocket.

I heard the door open.

— I am in…. What do you need?

— I need you to walk around the garage.

As soon he put his foot on the next piece of the floor...

I heard the explosion!

I called Giuseppe and informed him about the accident!

He sent two big guys to clean the evidence, then send that guy to the hospital and paid him to stay quiet.

It is morning and I am driving toward Laura's house before school opens.

I stopped the scooter in front of Laura's house, waiting until she comes out of the door.

Saw her parents leave the house walking towards their car.

They left, a few minutes after I saw her.

I took my helmet and held it against her head.

— How could you do that to me? I start crying.

She was the only one who could really hurt me; she has one part of my heart.

For a moment, I thought about our 15 years together, those beautiful memories together, then that explosion in the garage,

— I could be Dead! What is wrong with you? My voice is raised. I am your sister, I involved you in this and I am so sorry, but I cannot stay a minute without you, Laura. I am lost without you...

We were best friends; she was like a sister to me.

People thought we were in relationship, because our fighting was like a couple when they argue about stupid things.

With tears on my eyes, I continued to tell her:

— I did not walk into that garage; it wasn't me. Would you really want to see my blood on the floor? I prefer you do it, no other people, you have the balls Laura!

I gave her my Berretta .92 and told her to kill me, look into my eyes until I was dead.

She could not hold that gun for even one moment!

Then she says...

— Do you understand that you will go in prison? Do you really want this for your life? Die behind the bars! Is that what you really want? What about our friendship? I want you at my 18th birthday party, when I will buy a car and when I will be a mother, I want my friend back. I don't know you any more, Vanessa! Who are you? My friend or a criminal? You get brainwashed by those gangsters. You have to choose. Me or them?

— Laura, listen, please don't ask me to do something I cannot do it. I am so involved now. I have a plan.

— Really? She starts getting very angry. You told me that already! No more excuses, Vanessa. Please go! Get out of my sight!

I am so upset, heartbroken and Laura... she was the only happy thing in my life. However, I had obligations with those criminals; I did want to stay with her, not with them.

I have decided to talk with Giuseppe about how I am feeling.

It is late evening, I am driving to his house.

I saw the sofa again, that sofa when I had that Sprite a long time ago,

Then I am sitting on that sofa again.

He is coming to see me, I am ready to talk.

— Vanessa, my love, how was school?

— Giuseppe, listen...

My legs are shaking, and I am getting nervous.

I talk as I cannot hold it in any more...

— I am not here to talk about the school, I am here because I don't feel comfortable any more to stay with you and your team. I am young, I want a better life, I am sorry, I want to get out of this. Kill me, if is that what you want...

— Vanessa, darling, putting his right hand on my shoulder. I don't want to hurt you or kill you, why are you saying that?

— Well, you already did! My mental health has been murdered since I have been working for you.

— If you don't want this life any more, it is OK, don't worry, I am not upset. I understand. I will talk to your Dad about his naughty daughter!

— Whatever! I do not care any more, please you can take back the car if you want!

As soon I stepped out the door, I called Laura.

— Hello? She answers.

— Hi, it's me, Are you ok?

— Where are you? I need to see you and give you some good news.

I walked to her house about 45 minutes away, smoking a few cigarettes while I was walking.

She is there, like the Groom waiting for his bride at the centre of the altar.

I smile, I look at her, then run towards her.

— I have done it! If is that what you want! I am out of this; I want to stay with you Laura. I choose you! Are we still friends? I added.

— She is crying.

— Come on, don't cry , you should be happy about it!

She cannot talk, Laura! Laura!

Then her voice:

— Vanessa, my father's shop, his shop...is...

— Laura please talk, what happens?

— His shop is gone!

— What do you mean gone?

— Someone put a bomb in his business, he is at the police station now.

I stopped talking, I took the scooter and drove to the shop. I got in although the firemen told me to keep out.

Everything is burning and the flames are too high to look for some evidence.

I walked behind, then noticed a motorbike that is going away from the store.

That motorbike was Giuseppe's bike.

Laura is sad and she didn't come to school for about a week; she also doesn't want to talk with me any more.

I went to Giuseppe's house.

I don't know who I am any more, what I want; I am walking in the middle of the street and I am losing my focus.

Who am I? I am asking this question to myself.

I open the front door of his house, and see him walk to the door

— I am here!

— Oh, what a surprise?

— Why did you set fire to Laura's Dad's store? She is my best friend, you knew that.

— Vanessa, remember, she was the one who put that bomb in the garage! This is not a friend; she must pay for it!

— Giuseppe, can you please stop being a judge? You think who must pay or not? Now she does not talk to my any more! Are you happy now? Do you think I will change my mind because I am by myself? I am not scared of being lonely.

Then his diabolic plan again; he opened a bottle of champagne and poured some drink on my glass. He is always doing this, when he is talking business.

— Vanessa, I see you care about Laura, I have a plan, as we are friends as well. We are friends, aren't we? I will give some money for your friend's house, enough money to make sure her Dad can re-open the business.

— Sure, what do you want from me now? I know you; I know you will not do nothing for nothing.

— Well, there is something that I need. One last job, a last favour. I need you to drive from one city to another and transport some people with you.

— Is it going to be the absolute last Job?

— Of course, consider as a favour for your friend Laura. Are you going to dry her tears with a tissue now? He said, smiling.

— Have a good night! I responded. Then I walked away.

The road is quiet, I stopped at a gas station, put some petrol in my scooter, thinking about my new life how would be later and start to look for a way to leave that dangerous life.

It is only 6 months more left at my GED, then I am free to plan my escape. So, I keep my mind set, and calm and I agreed to do my last job for him.

I have enough money to buy a house, going abroad, maybe study in New York, a lot of dreams are coming to my mind, and a positive feeling to go and run away from that city.

Until when Laura texted me:

— Vanessa, I have received some money from Giuseppe. What does he want from you? What has he asked you this time? I don't think I can accept this money.

I respond Laura:

— Please keep the money, I will do anything for you, I will die for you! Don't worry, leave to me, I am on it! Goodnight.

She responds:

— Vanessa, do you remember when my Dad went to the police station last time, to report the crime? The officer told him that there is an online application to join the police! I think it could save your ass from everything!

I texted back:

What? Me in the police? Are you crazy? Go to sleep. Talk tomorrow.

She texted back:

— Listen to me, I will help you apply, then they will send you far away from Sicily, it is good for you, is also a good salary...You already know how to use a gun , don't you? 😊 You said you will do anything for me!

— It's late! Let's go to sleep. Night

It is March 2008, Saturday night.

I am driving a van from Tirana to Italy...

Inside the van are two guys from Albania; I am taking them from the border to Sicily.

Each guy is paying about ten thousand Euros to get into Italy. A guard at the check point by the border was already in agreement with Giuseppe.

But that guard was not there this time.

I have five kilos of cocaine in the trunk, hidden inside the spare tyre.

Fifty thousand euros in cash and three guns.

The guard told me to stop.

I smiled, being normal with him; I try not to look suspicious.

I am already thinking about my life behind bars for about 20 years, thinking about a good lawyer, thinking about my Mum, my grandparents, people who loved me, who turn my negative days in positive ones, then me.

Stupid, I am a loser, I am exchanging my life for money, I am stupid!

I think that's it! This is what I deserve! This is how my life will end.

I stopped the van, gave my ID to the guard. The guard is calling a dog for an inspection.

My heart is stopping, I will never forget that day!

That day I was the luckiest person in the world!

Suddenly, behind my van there is a truck with a family. Behind this truck the guard has noticed some people hidden. They ran away!

The guard told me to switch on the van and go, giving back my passport!

He apologized to me as well. I smiled and sayd, that is ok! Have a nice day!

I lit up a cigarette and looked back to the road from the mirror. I was lucky, God was with me, Laura as well, I guess.

I took the Albanians to Giuseppe's house, then as usual the envelope!

He was surprised to see me.

I walked to his door and stopped by the mat, as we agreed the job is done.

I didn't mention about that the guard was not there. That was his plan!

He was trying to make me vanish with that favour. I took the envelope. Five thousand euros, inside, not a penny more. Of course, he didn't think that I was coming back to Sicily.

It is one month at my GED and I am focusing on my studying whiling try to join the Police as well.

Laura was acting differently with me. She was pushing me every day to join the Police.

She was stopping me in the middle of the school, in the toilet, in the store, saying:

— Vanessa, I don't see your name in the list?

Did you apply for it or not yet? Her pressure was like my mother's pressure when she wants me to get the GED.

I stopped one afternoon in her house with my passport and my personal details.

I ring her doorbell. I am ready! I said.

She opened the door and she helped me complete the application, not because she wanted to help me only, she wanted proof. Yes, she has to be sure her friend Vanessa has finished the application and that it will be submitted.

As soon we received the email. The Application was submitted...

She hugged me saying:

— I will pray for you, they will accept you, I am confident!

Six months later I had passed the GED.

Got an email, saying that I was successful!

I went to Rome for my interview. I passed the exams and the different tests, then the check my height, my mental health, then a general body check.

They are asking me if I smoke or drink or use drugs.

My test is fine!

Two weeks later an envelope arrived.

Ms Nocera Vanessa, we would like to inform you that your application has been successful therefore, we would like to invite you to pack your luggage and attend your first day in the Military Police Training based in Rome.

We look forward to welcoming you on board,

Kind regards,

The Military Police Team

After getting that letter, all my family was very proud of me!

My mum organized a Party and Laura and I drunk so much that time, that I fell into the swimming pool and although she wasn't that drunk, she joined me!

Telling me: If you jump, I will jump with you because you are my friend!

One week later, I bought the bus ticket to Rome, one way.

Two weeks later, I was wearing a Uniform, and had a gun.

Military life and Aviano Air Base

Standing outside my dorm, it is late at night. I feel the wind across my hair. I have decided to light up a cigarette; that strong smell gets to the window of my co-worker; he joins me straight away.

— Are you Vanessa? he asked. From Sicily?

I gaze at him.

— Yes, I am; why?

— Nice to meet you, I am Fabio.

— You are popular here, I heard you were the best pool table-woman player in Sicily...

— Well, I am not good anymore like before, but I can still play.

— There is a pool table over the American side, shall we go there? It is only 10 minutes' walk...

I pause; my eyes are looking at his lips and he looks back at mine.

I have only seen him twice in the Canteen.

But he was a very handsome guy.

Fabio, late twenties, from Naples, a common Italian fashion guy; his cheeks are chiselled like a finely carved Michelangelo statue. His nose is perfectly symmetrical. His lips are slightly full: the kind that end in a cute little smirk at the corners.

— OK! Sure, Let's go!

Walking together for those 10 minutes was a nice sensation as a female Airman.

It was the first week in Aviano for me after my military training with only females over a period of 8 weeks.

From the edge of the road I saw the bar.

American flags were everywhere, and a Harley Davidson parked outside surrounded by Ford Mustangs.

There was a distinct smell of American perfume around the place.

A mix of Victoria's Secret body spray and Busch Beer.

Short skirt American girls talking about daily bullshit, walking like they don't care.

I get into the bar, reaching the pool table.

I was distracted by another good-looking guy.

He was playing pool with a couple of friends.

I saw him.

An Indian looking guy, tattoos over his arms, rosary neck-less and a NY hat.

A bull tank.

He was wearing Michael Jordan's shoes.

Is it possible that an Indian guy looks so American?

His eyes, very deep brown, beautiful eyes, look like Mascara was on, but that was the natural long size of his eyelashes, making me already more than interested,.

Oh my God, is he watching me at my table?

Fabio is there, he saw a cheeky smile crossing my lips.

He pauses… Vanessa? That guy is keeping looking at you, do you like him?

— Who?

— Come on Vanessa, don't be chilly.

— Not really my cup of tea, I answer

I lied, of course; I want to maintain my professionalism in the Airbase.

But it was evident.

Fabio talked to him.

Music is loud and people are talking, too noisy to understand what he is saying but I understand the body language.

I saw him walking towards me.

Is coming to me? On my own think: OK Vanessa, relax, you can talk in English, can't you?

Well, I only studied it at the High School, having a teacher that was interested only in Harrods store and red buses, and why did I learn it? Because I like Harrods or the red buses?

The previous teacher was cool, she could engage the class, she had the power to take all of us into the imagination of the adventure of Lochness.

Lochness?

I always had a feeling that the Monster was living there, maybe because the lake was dark, like getting lost in a deep dark sky of 3am.

But I always was interested in learning English.

Eminem was my favourite rapper, a point of reference, especially when the movie 8 Mile was out.

I was 12, when my Mum took me to the cinema, for my birthday.

She was waiting outside for me.

— Vani, how was the movie? I remember she asked.

I could not express my enthusiasm when I watched it.

— Yes, mum, was good, thanks.

I was always attractive from the street life of the American Gangster, especially Eminem, a white rapper!

— OK, I think I am ready to talk, OK come down, I know you can do it! Just stop talking to myself.

He stands at me.

— Hi, I am Elvis, he says. Nice to meet you! What is your name?

I gaze at him. Oh my God! Is it a miracle? Is just like a dream come true!

I could smell the Johnson's baby cream for a second, coming from his skin, no it was not that smell. What was it? Palmers cocoa butter lotion, that smell was cocoa butter!

I smile, Elvis?

— Yes? He answers.

— Like Elvis Presley?

— Yes! I would love to play with you, he says... come with me, let's have some drink first.

He holds my hand.

He took me to the bar; I was thinking to order a Jack and Coke...

The atmosphere is chilled, people are dancing, laughing.

He invites me to dance.

I was not that drunk, I don't know this song.

He says:

— Just go through the left when say left!... and to the right when the DJ says right!

Wow! I am in the middle of the bar... with so many different people, and I try to copy them... This is the first time I am dancing to this song!

It is a very popular American song.

— The Cupid Shuffle, he says, down down do your dance. No worries you will be ready next time when you next come back!

The DJ plays it every Friday night.

We are walking through the bar.

— Excuse me Sir! Could you give us 2 Jager Bombs?

— Sure! the Bartender answers.

I never forget what the Bartender looked like; big scar on his bold hair and dark eyes, a very big guy; when I was looking at him, couldn't stop thinking about Uncle Fester of the Adams Family.

I stop.

I am thinking what was inside this cocktail; is it a cocktail? With Red Bull?

Confusing my thinking up and down, Elvis paid the bill, 13 boxes, that stand for dollars.

— Are you teasing me? He says. Come on, don't you know what Jager Bombs are?

I paused; of course it is Jägermeister and Red Bull.

Just because I had seen the Bartender pour it previously.

He smiles. So I heard you are a good pool player.

— Do you know how to play bank?

I smile; yes, I play bank as well.

We are starting to play, Handball few times for me.

This means open table, you can play the white ball where you want, 5 stripes balls on the table, all of them in the hole straight away.

He was shocked!

And his eyes were more beautiful than before!

I cannot stop looking at him and imagine the feeling of how would be to have sex with him on this pool table!

I start to get into the feeling of having a dirty mind while I was playing.

I won the first game.

His friends teasing him.

We were still drinking, when I saw Fabio that was flirting with 2 Americans.

I called him.

— Fabio! Fabio, I'm leaving.

Fabio is coming to me....

— OK I am coming with you, let's go! Vanessa? So how was the game with Elvis?

— It was good thanks, but why you talking to him about me, without checking first....

I was upset, happy upset...

He gazes at me, Vanessa, I gave him your number.... sorry I hope you didn't mind

— What? How could you? At least double check with me?

I was not upset because he gave him my number, I was just wondering how to communicate with him and writing in English...

— Ok, fine! But next time please ask me!

We are reaching the steps of the dorm.

I was on a second floor; he stops on the first floor, looking at me.

— You are a good pool player, he says, and Hot!

I bite my lips and giving him a spontaneous kiss on his cheek.

— Goodnight Fabio! See you tomorrow!

— Goodnight Vanessa!

In my dorm, on my bed, I'm still thinking about Elvis.

His neckless was a rosary, I was thinking how it would feel kissing his rosary over his skin…

His body over my body!

A mystery world, full of passion, different cultures, different lifestyle.

I checked my phone.

1 New Message.

New number starting with 001-201…

I was sleepy… And I just saw:

Hi Vanessa! This is Elvis! I really enjoyed play pool with you, maybe we can play again next Friday? Goodnight!

I am replying:

Hi Elvis, I am happy that you enjoyed, sure text me the time that you will be there, and I will try my best to be there! Goodnight!

I was thinking about Fabio for a second, this wouldn't have happened if he didn't give Elvis my phone number.

It is early morning and I am late for the Anthem.

Yes, is Saturday, and 8am, actually 08:01.

I am late of 1 minute.

Everyone looked at me as they though I was 10 minutes late!

There is something that I hate about the military; the first year you are committed to sing the National Anthem, looking the Flag rising up the edge of the Building and wake up every morning for the 365 days and walking 5 minutes to reach the Square when you will admire the flag and sing with a consistent voice and if you missed it, you have to help the officer with the toilets cleaning or helping out the higher soldier in rank in what they need during the day!

I was tired! I slept about 2 hours, my eyes were tired, and the officer came to me.

— Nocera!

— Yes Sir! I say.

— 25 Push-Ups! You were late!

I nod my head and drop to the floor…

It was the hottest day and the floor was burning.

I spit into the palms of my hands, I was thinking of a torture for him, but this would not be helping me with the push-ups.

I started my first 15, my arms shaking; it feels the vibration on the warm floor,

This officer was nearly thirties, bold hair, and sunglasses that you cannot dare to look into his eyes expression.

He saw that I was struggling to continue. He put his left boot on my neck pushing downwards to the floor, telling me, you are not a female, you are a soldier! Go away! Now!

I was feeling raped for a minute, without being touched!

I went upstairs in my room again.

I was thinking how it would be in the other side of the Airbase.

Aviano Airbase was in Pordenone, North of Italy.

Piancavallo is a ski resort in the Dolomites.

Every Soldier who was assigned to Aviano Air base visited Piancavallo.

Sunsets in Aviano are like postcards that you buy from the store, and every moment you miss your family or you feeling a bit down, every move you take, the landscape is like it is talking to you, a huge mountain surrounded by sunlight, blue sky and white snow creating vibrations of emotion in your heart, making you feel blessed that you are there.

That was the only thing I really enjoyed about.

Aviano was not in my plan, the officer decided my destination during the training and I really could not change his mind. He thought that experience of the countryside far away from my family will be a good experience for me in order to make me grow more. I was not happy when I arrived there, I had to carry three pieces of luggage to the second floor by myself and the boys just looking behind following after me; they only person who asked me if I need help with my belongings was Fabio.

I was the second Female Airman in all the Italian Air base and all the soldiers tried to flirt with me, during the performance of the National Anthems; during lunch time or during the running competitions. However, they are good looking boys, once you fall into one soldier, you will be popular not because you win a medal but because you are too easy to get.

I was there only to achieve my goals, and having an extra point for my CV, so I was able to continue to join the Police later. I was not interested in flirting as I had already a plan in mind and if I would flirt, I might be more interested in new experience, such as going through the American Side of the Base and find the guy for me there!

The Airbase is divided in two sides: Italian Side and American Side

The Italian dorms were very old, dark green wall, nobody was looking after the lawns, metal wardrobes in the accommodations, spiders on the floor, mosquitoes around your room and the toilets, well, the toilets were OK, 3 showers and 3 sinks.

I had a rota with the other girl, and we were sharing the bathroom and corridor cleaning as well.

She was married and focusing on her carrier. She was a very meticulous person; in her spare time, she was interested only in exercising and studying.

One time, I decided to invite her to come to a party. I introduced my friend Fabio to her. She had a couple of drinks and she was kissing Fabio and letting him touch her big breasts.

I was thinking she was having fun for her first time; she was really enjoying the night. I was quite happy for her as she was a classic housewife that looks after the husband and prepares the dinner getting ready to listen to parents problems. I was feeling guilty at the beginning because I was aware of her marriage, but she was happy for her first time. I never saw her smiling and laughing like that, so, why would I feel guilty? At the end is her life and she is mature enough to understand her limits.

Her name was Maria, she was 5.6 feet tall with curly hair and had a very good shape. She was wearing blue jeans that night and a white top. We get back into the dorms again. The moon is huge and there are stars everywhere; she holds my hand and she look me into my drunk eyes, telling me:

— Vanessa, I am so lucky to have you here in my life, since I met you my life in Aviano has been changed!

— Well, Maria… I think, you deserve to be happy! I say.

Being a soldier is a mix of feeling, one day you miss home, the other day is like you feel at home!

I hug her and waiting for her to reach her door, reaching my door in the meantime.

Lie dying on my bed and thinking about the night with a hot camomile, my eyes shut immediately.

It is Friday morning. I have been checking my phone since 3 days; no text message from Elvis, I hate the feeling when you check your phone every five minutes, looking to see if he has text you; wishing in a small tone and see the number that you want to see. I also want to be sure that the Wi-Fi was working so I check it.

The Network was fine, the connection was fine! I was hoping for a text from Elvis all day, but I received nothing. I was a bit upset so I text Fabio to see what he was doing. I wanted to go out, I wanted to forget about the disappointment of no message. Fabio was in his room. He invited me to a party, an American Party! I was hoping to see Elvis at it, so I decided to wear a yellow dress that night with silver heels and a silver clutch.

Fabio has a Mercedes, so I wasn't too worried about walking or not drinking alcohol as he was driving. We reached the Club. The music is loud, Security at the gate, Hip-hop and Reggae tonight they mention, I look Fabio into his eyes, I nod at him as I wanted to check the club and what is in there, yes, we get in. We reach the Bar. We had a couple of shots of Jack Daniels.

I started to feel drunk and was dancing close to him; his hands are following my moving and we are laughing and enjoying the music and keeping a few shots on the side for later. The atmosphere is perfect and we both look stunning, getting the attention of the Americans, they look at us like when are different, is a funny way that I like about Americans, they don't care about fashion or matching the top with the shoes and the bag with the jeans, they are just comfortable, I would say too comfy for my style.

I am not a fan of big brands like Gucci, Chanel, or D&G but I love to spend time on matching the colour with the clothes.

I am in the middle of the Disco club, enjoying my dance. A guy came to me asking, if Fabio was my Boyfriend, I said yes, he is my Boyfriend.

Giving a cheeky kiss to Fabio on his lips. The guy left and walked away.

— Vanessa? Fabio says. What a lovely surprise from you! How beautiful it is! Can I have another? he says.

— Fabio please, it was just to make that guy walked away! I say.

But he was not happy about my answer and suddenly, he kissed me again and again, such as a magnet all night, we couldn't stop touching each other.

We left the Club, the car was in the parking space and start raining and I didn't care to get wet because Fabio was there holding my hand, kissing me passionately under the open sky, lost in a bubble of time and space, we not even noticing the heavy waterfalls pouring down over our body while we were getting soaking wet.

We decided to continue the night together in his room. He took off his T-shirt, his body was perfect, right muscles at the right point. He offered me a foot massage.

I was super-tired and fell asleep on his chest. I was feeling safe with him and supported. We slept together all night without thinking about having sex. We took off our clothes and were naked under the blankets, holding each other tight like two bodies turning into one and that's how we fell asleep.

Fabio was always part of my life in all my military career; we had missions together.

We had been in different places together and although we had always been attracted to each other, we never had the right time or the effort to dedicate more of that feeling on just us.

We were ready to protect the world together and we would always be the Leaders in the team, pushing each other to achieve goals, ambitions, and dreams.

He left me with a lot of good memories which are much better than photographs as they are safe in my mind and I can see and feel them whenever I want. Those moments were very emotional for me.

When I finished my training, I was ready to settle down with Fabio. Unfortunately, my plan was changed; another call, this time from NATO, asking me to be posted for six months in Afghanistan.

I kept Fabio's picture in my wallet for the entire six months.

But up of my return, I found that with the passage of time, life change, people change, and plans change as well.

As soon as I left my final mission, I was trying to call him. He wasn't in the military any longer; his dream came true, he made it!

He was finally in the FBI, that was Fabio's goal.

Of course, I was happy for him, but at the same time I was sad as I knew I had lost him.

I lost an opportunity, like you lose that special train that only passes once in your life!

I lost that opportunity to tell him about my feelings because I was scared or embarrassed.

I was not ready before but when I was ready for him, he was no longer there for me.

Fabio will be always in my heart; he also saved my life once when we had a firearms training.

And that picture is still in my wallet!

Elvis

I will never forget those nights when I used to work at Gate 9. Gate 9 was the worse shift ever in the Air Force. Working for 24 hours in one shift. Yes, 24 hours on, then 24 hours off! Many times, I thought torture must surely be better than Gate 9. The shift started in the morning, at 9am. You must check ID for 3 hours and inspect every vehicle going in or out. Check documents are registered in the airbase and ensure the health and safety of the space. At 12 someone would pick me up and take me to the canteen for lunch. Then training for an hour in the training room; like a briefing with the team then you go back again at 3pm to finish at 6pm, have some dinner and go back at 9pm until Midnight. At midnight you can rest for a few hours but only on one condition; you cannot remove your boots and the bullets must always remain on your belt; then the last 3 hours, from 3am to 6am. In that time, you will feel tired, nervous, hungry but you still need to be vigil and ensure you protect the entrance to the base. So, I decided to take coffee with me and few cigarettes that I can sneakily light up once everything was really quiet. The shift was very organized: one Italian, two Americans.

The funniest thing about working with them was to have some fried egg and peanut butter left over around 4am and after a long shift you cannot wait until that time because you are too tired to think and it is cold outside, especially in winter. The Americans were always nice to me and they treated me with respect every time we shared a shift together. It is Friday, 3 am in the morning, the temperature is minus 15, and I have to stay outside by the gate far away from the heater. I can't feel my feet anymore, can't talk properly; I can only look at the soldiers coming by the gate and checking their ID with my gloves and with my scarf over my neck. I saw a BMW coming through me, I am ready for the check point. Check point procedures were quite strict, as you also need to check the alcohol level of the driver. If the result is positive you must handcuff him and wait until the police arrive for the arrest procedures and other paperwork. Can you imagine arresting someone at 4am in the morning and then talking with them about police after you have stood for about 22 hours. It not really easy as you reach a point that you are tired and you lose concentration and have trouble with true perception of the reality; the only thing that you are thinking of is your bedroom and a hot drink. However, that night was different. As soon I pulled over the BMW at the check point I can see that guy was familiar to me, he was looking tired and with my sleepy eyes I asked him for his ID. I checked his ID and the picture, of course I know that guy! It is Elvis!

He was looking cool and immaculate in his uniform. Immediately I forgot about my 23Hours of shift and the only thing that I remember was the adrenaline rush of excitement.

It was all coming back to me; the blood, yes, my blood was circulating properly again, I was feeling normal and fresh again, such a sunlight was there heating the surface of my skin.

— Vanessa! The pool player! He starts saying.

— Hi Elvis! How are you?

It has been long time since I did not hear from you.... I thought you were going to confirm the time that Friday night!

I am so sorry, I flew to Spain for a mission of 2 weeks, I came back yesterday, and I was very busy with the training, please forgive me! You don't deserve my silence!

(Distance doesn't separate people, silence does.)

In my mind....

What about if we go for a drink tomorrow?

Tomorrow? I gaze at him; I was thinking in my mind about Sunday that could be more suitable, but I was so into him that, suddenly I say

— Yes! That's fine!

— What time? I added

— 4pm.

Well I might still in bed for 4 pm but yes why not?

I return the ID to him, touching his hands with my gloves!

He moved the car and drove back then he turned and went away from the gate, waving his hands from his window.

My colleague, the American, noticed my suddenly happy face; he saw me smiling on my own and asked me if I was ok. Oh yes! I was feeling excited about that shift!

That Gate which I used to hate so much, had now given me the opportunity to start dating the guy that I was into,

I cannot believe that in about 10 hours I will be with my Elvis once again!

I am thinking about my nails and my hair; so, I booked a manicure and pedicure straight away! I didn't think about resting as I had too much adrenaline energising me during the day; so I dedicated my time in choosing what dress to wear, what shoes and which bag.....so the morning is going to be busy getting everything ready and perfect before our official date.

It is 3.45 in the afternoon and I am ready; I have done my hair and my make-up, then a text.

Hi Vanessa, I am on way will be by your dorm at 4pm.

I have a big smile when seeing the text. Then I finish putting on my perfume.

While I am drinking a coffee, he rings me and telling me that he is downstairs waiting for me. He was wearing a black t-shirt, jeans and Michael Jordan shoes, same rosary over his neck and tattoo crossing his arms. He hugged me; not those long hugs that you wish to enjoy, one of those quick hugs just for few seconds. He starts: Hey How you doing?

You look amazing! He added.

Well, it took me about 3 hours to choose the right outfit for that special occasion.

He starts to turn on the car and with his cheeky eyes, he is looking at me all the time.

I am feeling good with him, the music is perfect and the atmosphere warm and his car quite comfortable. He put on the heater on the back of my seat and asked me if I am feeling cold; he was very protective that day with me. He drove to until we reached the Bar.

Here we are, he says.

He opened my door, holding my hand!

Oh, thanks, I respond.

The bar is by the mountain; he booked a place on the terrace that you could see the sunset from the windows.

He removed my coat and took with his to leave with the bartender.

Then he ordered a bottle of wine, and some olives with some chicken wings.

We began drinking, and getting to know each other. He told me that he is origins are Indian from Pakistan and that he grew up in New York City. He left home when he was 18 years old and he has been in the air force for about 4 years. He is very happy to stay in Europe because his plan was to visit Italy, France, Germany, and Malta. He added that his contract will be another 2 years longer then he must return to the States.

I told him about myself, my ambitions, my goals. However, as my English was not very fluent, he tried to help me to talk when he saw I was struggling with some words. *Speak*

It took me about 20 minutes just to say where I was from and what drink I usually like!

Yes, this is how everything starts.

He was curious about my lifestyle; I wish I could talk more; I want to talk but I cannot.

Yes, I was struggling and embarrassed.

Smoking a cigarette outside he asked me if I like the sunset. Yes, I do love the sunset when you can admire the Landscape of Piancavallo.

He mentioned about his balcony and the stunning mountain views he gets just in front of his eyes; so with a cheeky smile I started to tell him:

It would be lovely to see it right now....

Of course, with few glasses of wine I was feeling not as shy as usual,

He got his car from the parking lot, paid the bill and we drove towards his House.

He still looking at me, I want to kiss him so bad...

His lips are soft and perfect, his cute smile crossing his cheeks, he was also about 6 feet, so I did feel good when I was walking with him into the main entrance of his house.

We are in the house.

His house was massive, the Air Base gave about one thousand dollars towards a rent to the American contractors and he was one of them.

There is a swimming pool in the garden, a pond with red fishes, a space dedicated to a relax area with a private bar, two showers by the pool and a tennis table by the parking.

He walked me in, and he gave me the grand tour of his home.

The living room was spacious enough for about 6 people.

The dining room was by the kitchen in like an open space between the living room and the kitchen. With 2 bathrooms, you might expect ok one of them will be just a very small one. Not at all, they were both were super huge, the only different was that one has the jacuzzi inside and another one shower with water-proof radio and speaker.

The house was super clean.

He shows me the bedroom. The bed was so high that you could injure yourself if you fell off. He took me onto the balcony. He bed set out two chairs and started telling me about the neighbourhood and the shops in the local area.

He handed me a glass of Jack Daniels and I added some coke on it; we are still chatting, then we moved inside.

Is about 9pm in the night,

And I started to feel tired, I know that I was off the next day, but I could not keep my eyes open.

He saw me chilling in his living room and he offered that I could stay over. But as a first date I feel I should not even be in his house. I was teasing telling him to see the sunset from his balcony....

He dropped me off at the base again.

Holding my hand, he asked me another date on Tuesday,

I must check my calendar I say, I will let you know.

I think it will be fine! But will confirm on Monday, I added.

He kissed me and from his pocket, he gave me a gift!

A gift? Wow, this is really kind of him, I think.

Open it when you arrive upstairs then let me know if you like it!

We kiss in his car by my dorms, with my elegant behaviour I thank him for the beautiful evening and walk away towards the steps of the main entrance.

I am in my room; I tear off the plastic paper and unpack the gift.

It was a perfume, Angel, with the shape of a star. Then a card says:

 I had the feeling to date an Angel and I was in the store and thought this will be the perfect fragrance for you as it has your name on it!

Love,

Elvis

I am a bit surprised but very happy at the same time.

I smoked my last cigarette and got ready for sleep.

It is Tuesday and I almost finish my shift! Elvis has offered to get some take- away then relax with him in his living room.

I place my bullets with the gun and complete my handover; then ran to my room for a shower to get ready for Elvis.

He picked me up at 11am, the airbase is busy. My Italian co-worker saw me going out of the base with an American; he started spreading the news around!

I did not really care about him. I am confident enough and if they want to gossip about me, that's okay. I think they must have a boring long shift if the only thing they do is talk about me. I let them do it as I wanted to focus on Elvis and had no time for distractions. I am in the car with him and everything feel so different he makes me feel safe and protected. I did not think about anything, the stress is far away from me and we start to think which takeaway order.

I would go for Italian he says,

I would go more for Chinese I say,

Fine! Let's get Chinese then! he added.

We get the food and some drinks, then we start proceeding towards the house.

We arrived, he parked, he opens the door and we start eating as I was starving!

We are sitting in the dining room. He started telling me about his favourite meal and I was very surprised how he could eat a fresh pepper with his food while talking normally with me. I do love spicy food but that was too hot for me! I decided to try it; I remember I spent ten minutes in the toilet drinking milk and starting to cry!

It is about 2 pm in the afternoon, we are chilling in the living room finishing the meal.

I offer to give him some help with the cleaning.

No, darling, relax and watch tv, he says.

Ok, then I looked at him and taking into consideration the word 'relax'.

I took off my shoes and with the noise of the washing machine on and his footstep around the kitchen while he was washing the dishes, I fall asleep.

I wake up open my eyes, slowly, I stop,

He was sitting next to me watching me while I was sleeping.

It is dark outside and from the window of the living room I can also see the stars.

Elvis? I say

What time is it?

It is 11pm darling, and you look very beautiful when you sleep, with a relaxing breathing he added.

Oh my God Elvis!

I must go back to the Base!

It is so late!

You can stay here he says.

I am so sorry Elvis I must get back to the base, as the officer will check if I am in the room every day around 11.30pm.

Can we be there before 11.20? I asked

Sure, get ready I will be waiting in the car for you!

There is something that I hate of the military, yes after the morning anthem you also need to confirm your present every day at 11.30 in the evening and if they notice that you are not in the room they can fire you or they will drop your score from excellent to good, of course Elvis was a very strong irresistible temptation for me but I also need to follow the policy of the base.

Therefore, as soon he stopped the car, I kiss him, and I start running to the dorms. I was so lucky.... the officer just passes my colleague room ready to know my room and luckily, I am there next to him at the right time.

He asked me how my day was and with my real smile I say, I was very busy with the training and I wish to pass the exam as I was busy studying!

Studying English with that American or studying for your career? He added.

He looked me in the eyes and says:

— You are very special and smart! When I was your age, I was in love with an American girl, her contract expires then she left me here and she had just used me.

Don't be his distraction! Unless you just want to have fun!

Don't be serious about being in relationship as they will dump you when you are not expecting to be dumped, he added.

I couldn't say even one word to all that as I was aware that Elvis's contract expired in two years' time and he was ready to leave when that time arrived.

But at the same time, I was really happy about our dating, he was always nice with me, why should I stay single and alone?

I am here on my own as well with no family and people that I don't really care about or to socialise with. They are all focussed on work then to get back to their rooms. I want to enjoy my time and my life here in Aviano Air base and getting to know the culture, the people, the mountain, travelling around, with Elvis this was possible, he was like me interested in discover new things and learn about the future, learn about something new all the time. Plus, he was cute, he made me feel happy and safe, and I was learning English with him, so why should I stop all this?

I love to live in the moment, and I am not thinking to get married, so I think to myself, why not enjoy the Military together with Elvis!

This time with Elvis was very special to me. I always have a strong opinion that the best way to learn a language is to start a friendship with a mother-tongue speaker. He was very patient with me and with a drink and a funny chat, I was starting to speak English better and better every day. I have to thank his consistent patience with me.

Elvis was the first person who gave me the best performance with the English, and after a couple of weeks I was talking faster.

I could now have a conversation at the Gate with the Americans!

They were also were aware that I was dating one of their men, so they began to give me more peanut butter; also they were nicer to me than before. Elvis always corrected me when I was talking,

Putting all his effort, explaining to me new synonyms and better way to pronounce a word, so I have to say a very big thank you to him and my American co-worker!

I also noticed that as soon as I started to speak English, Gate 9 was no longer in my list of placements. My team were very envious that I was working in the office, looking after translations, as I was given the opportunity to translate American documents into Italian and ensure that all the data was up do date.

I was very pleased with my achievement and for the relationship with Elvis helping me achieving my goals.

That beautiful period was one of many more to arrive.

Although I have my success in my life, I was not feeling complete. I needed to be next to a person like Elvis and so after we were dating for about a month, he began asking me if I would like to spend a weekend with him.

I decided to take 2 days off, so I didn't have to rush in the dorms to confirm my presence.

Elvis was always getting weekends off; therefore, I packed my suitcase to take with me what I needed and the essential clothes to spend a weekend away!

I was in a good mood. Elvis picked me up and from Pordenone we went to Slovenia, spend the night there, with him, I didn't worry too much about booking or confirmations he was thinking about everything; he booked an Hotel called the Landscape,

— Darling, are you ok? He asked.

Never feeling better, I answered.

He starts touch me over my underwear while is driving.

Then he took off his trousers, and he say:

Is only 15 minutes' drive to the Hotel babe,

But we were too much in love to wait.

We stopped the car in an emergency space in the highway.

He starts touch me then we moved to the back sit of the car and he starts touching me over my leg, licking me on my neck, I have very strong feelings with him, my fantasy was too huge to being satisfied.

He paused, then he says:

— I know what you want! Get off of the car, just keep your shoes.

In the empty highway you can just hear wolf in the forest, wolf howls, crickets everywhere, then our moan, following from our sweat.

I wasn't easy to be satisfied, well, I never was satisfied like I really want it.

That guy, he can make me scream and moan over and over because he never stops, maybe because he was working out every day and also led a healthy life, well, not too healthy as he was drinking and drinking every day!

We saw the Hotel from the edge of the road. As soon we stored our luggage in the room, we could not stop kissing and kissing each other.

For me he was difficult to trust someone especially after all my experiences in the past but not only that, it is not just about trust!

That feeling came naturally to me after several relationships in Sicily, before I joined the air force, that was the first time that I was feeling in Love.

Because I let myself to be loved by someone.

I opened my heart without thinking about what is next, the future and the family, the wedding etc...

The most common mistake when we start dating someone is to be worried about what is next and we never focus on the moment!

That moment!

The moment that takes us away from negativity and stress.

Dear readers, that time was my time! Finally, the time that I was waiting for....

Love is dangerous, you never understand this feeling but you know that you are totally immersed in it when you cannot stop thinking about that person, when you desire to kiss and hug that person, when you know that that person can read your mind even without speaking, because love is magic, magic like a kiss, magic like a lovely cuddle, and you know that you are in love when you don't see any imperfections of your loving partner!

He is your champion, your best friend, your dad, your brother, he is there to support you and give you motivation to achieve your goals, be calm when you are nervous, showing care when you are busy with other things.

Holding each other's hands.

— I think to myself for the first time... what a wonderful world!

That night I thought about men has been changed and I understand that even if you are heartbroken or your ex-boyfriend did not deserve you because he is loser that does not mean all men are the same. There is always that opportunity outside waiting for you and you just have to wait for your time, you just need to be at the right place at the right time, this is possible, if has not happened, it doesn't mean it will not happen.

Everyone has a weakness in their personality and my common weakness is impatience.

Because, I had everything I wanted to have, friends were there for me anytime I called them they always came running for me, not because I was Vanessa but because I was a boss involved in the Mafia, they could get scared if I was kept waiting too long

I know, it is difficult to change when you are old, therefore you don't need to change but to improve that part or that weakness trying to ensure an opportunity that will make that part of yourself better. Work on it every day and let your partner know about your dark side, so he could also give you some feedback and make you understand what you should work and not.

Elvis was a big part of my life, with his love he made me forget about my Dad, my past and finally I was feeling free. It is like you pay your price then you know you have freedom after.

Yes, I was free, and I was in love.

That weekend away, changed my opinion about people and love and I didn't regret one single moment spent with him because he was the one who cleared away the scar over my heart with all his love and his personality until one day....

The day when his contract expires, and he had to return to the States.

He began to act differently with me; he was very confused, then we decided to see how things could go together in the States; so I packed my luggage and flew over there.

New York was very different compared to Europe. Healthy food is overpriced, and rubbish food is very cheap. It is a very expensive city especially if you drive to downtown.

Anything and everything is possible there. There are different job offers, a monthly rent is about 3.000,00 Euros, it is the city that never sleeps, the lights will inspire you, it is divided in 5 districts – Brooklyn, The Bronx, Queens, Manhattan and Long Island. It was beautiful to live there but as soon as I met his family there were a few arguments.

I do love and respect Indian culture,

But don't force me to do something that I am not keen to do.

Elvis's mother took me to the shopping mall not to buy me a dress but to buy me a Sari.

When you are in love you will do anything for that person. I did not realize at that time my Italian culture was being turned into an Indian one. I didn't understand why Indian people run away from India to raise a family in New York keeping their strong traditions, just as though they are still in India; going to Indian restaurant, wearing a Sari around Manhattan, socialising only with Indian friends and relatives. If you are travelling around new countries, new places, it is good to meet other cultures, share new experiences.

I am open-minded and I absolutely love to try different types of food but every single day we used to eat basmati as the first course and chicken as the second course with some appetisers called Samosa and Pakora. The food was very spicy, but I did enjoy it.

The Indian weddings are very nice, but woman and man never dance close to each other, as long you cook, and you look after the house you are a perfect bride.

I wasn't there in New York to learn how to cook Chicken Biryani. I was there for Elvis, for our Love and a job opportunity for us that can raise our love even higher. .

My plan was to stay happy with him and with a job.

But his mother was always in the way between us. I have tried to talk to her, but she was too narrow-minded to make her understand my thoughts

It wasn't a good idea to move to New York; his mother tried to convince me to marry her son, so they organized an engagement party.

I spoke with Elvis about that; there was too much pressure on my shoulder,

I felt in an impossible position. I decided to return to Italy.

I broke up the relationship with Elvis. I had big hopes for us, but you cannot live your life on hopes alone.

A year later, I tried to apply to join the Italian FBI; my experience was strongly taken in consideration. I decided to think more about my life and my personal goals.

My application was successful, so I began to travel around Europe again until when Elvis called me that he wants to re-join the Air force and follow my destinations with the security job.

As we had been together for so much time and spent about six years together, I could not refuse his offer. He came to Italy first; we had few meetings before, then we tried to schedule our missions to match our destinations together.

Everything was back to normal, until he was called for a mission in Afghanistan (Kabul).

He stayed there for about six months; how he survived that mission was a miracle.

All his co-workers died in an explosion, he was injured but he survived; when he was with me, he didn't want to talk about that.

He spent most hours of each day drinking Jack Daniels and watching tv. He was drunk at 11 in the morning sometime. I had enough. So, I decided to pay for a mental help therapist. According to the therapist, he had depression caused not just from the explosion, but he could never tell me that in that mission he killed a four-year old child who was carrying bombs strapped to her stomach.

Unfortunately, the situation got worse.

It is a year since Elvis last worked and he is drunk every day. He refused my help; he didn't want to move on at all. I spent all the yearlong, supporting him financially. I did try to push him for a job and to visit the doctor once a week.

He started to use heroin as well; although I had a hard life, I had never killed a child.

I understood the pain in his heart, but life needs to continue. I couldn't think about him as a fiancé anymore. He felt down every day for more than a year and he could not get better. I tried to convince him to visit the psychiatrist again to focus on his mental health. In the meantime, I was late with my period.

I was under a lot of stress because I was supporting both of us, working hard, trying to get double shift every weekend to make more money and pay the therapist as well, so maybe that was the reason.

I argued with him as I was crazy at work then he wastes the money in alcohol and drugs so I thought to take it easy with him otherwise my life will go into that tunnel again.

It is morning, after my jogging section I bought the pregnancy test.

It is positive.

I wasn't ready to have a babe.

Especially with a father who is a heroin addict and not responsible as he was before.

During the evening I showed him the pregnancy test result during dinner and telling him about the news.

I still can change my mind and keep the baby, but he told me that he prefers to go back to New York and stay with his family.

It has been two weeks since I found out I am pregnant. A friend who was a gynaecologist, knew my situation, and gave me three pills, very strong pills, that would make me abort.

I realised after that episode, I started to fall again into the black moon.

I talked to the therapist and she convinced me to accept the thing that if the relationship is over, it was not my fault and she made me more focused on personal goals again, setting some new strong challenges to achieve to keep my mind distracted from Elvis.

I took a break from him, as I was trapped 24/h a day with his depression.

I stopped talking with my family. I stopped going out with friends. I stopped smiling.

As soon I stepped away from Elvis, I saw a life still going on outside, the world, the beauty of this earth. I came back to the house after a couple of days. That time away was important for me to think and make the right choice.

I saw him on the sofa' as usual, finishing a bottle of Jack Daniel, then telling me:

— Hey, where have you been?

— I took some time to think, I say.

— Elvis, listen, I am sorry if I am not strong enough to support you. What do you want to do in your life? What will make you happy? I am happy with you, he says.

Elvis, you have changed so much, you have improved as well, but I think Europe is not good for you anymore, you deserve to be next to your family. Someone who will look after you every day, someone who control you as you are weak at this time.

From the next day, he stopped drinking.

He booked a ticket one way for NYC in a week's time.

It is the departure day, I made some pasta for him, to take with him on the plane.

I dropped him off at the airport and tried to say a lot of positive words to make him feel good and proud of himself. He stopped before the security gate, kissed me and hugged me for about five minutes; although he was a drug addict, he did truly love me the whole time.

As soon I saw him leave the security gate, I received a text from him said:

Thanks for everything you did for me. I am on the plane, will text you when I am in New York.

I replied: Don't worry, I look forward to receiving your text, have a safe trip.

That day was the last time I ever saw him.

As soon I began to drive, I had tears on my eyes thinking about our beautiful relationship together.

Eight years together. He was my first love and my last love as I did not find a person like him again.

I did not regret a single moment of my time with him.

Although we don't talk any more as before, he will always remain in my heart.

I respect him and I thank him for everything he did for me, good and bad. Not as a delusion but as a very good experience of my life that helping me grow in a lot of aspects of my mind and the way to see things. Elvis now is an IT head manager, is working in New York and he has a life back again. This is what is important, he is safe and happy with his career.

Money laundering

Money laundering is a crime. It is usually described as the process of turning the proceeds of crime into property or money that can be accessed legitimately without arousing suspicion. The term 'laundering' is used because criminals turn 'dirty' money into 'clean' funds which can then be integrated into the legitimate economy as though they have been acquired lawfully. Money laundering comprises three distinct stages:

• Placement - movement of criminal proceeds from their source. For example, cash proceeds from crime may be paid into a bank or used to buy goods, property, or assets. Where is this money going? Getting rid of dirty money; as soon you pass this step the second step will be easy to achieve.
• Layering - undertaking transactions to conceal the origin of the money. For example, goods or other assets may be resold or funds transferred abroad.

Or in simple words:

washing the money with commercial transaction, just to make difficult the tracking of this activity, where this money is going

You can do plenty of things as soon you pass the first step, you can walk into a casino, or buy some gold and get a receipt.

• Integration - movement of laundered money into the economy so that it looks as if the money came from legitimate sources. For example, invoices from a 'front' company may be paid using cash. which originated as the proceeds of crime. Laundered cash can also be loaned to such a company.

Integrations: spending the clean cash, how? Easy.

Invest in property, buy an expensive car, buy some business shares, invest in a way that nobody will notice.

Malta is one of the most popular places for money laundering, followed by Switzerland and Iran.

Since I know Giuseppe, the common source for money laundering activities are, extortion, dodgy deals, criminal activities, prostitution, drug dealing, frauds, firearm selling.

A huge amount of money must be laundering into a final transaction.

Criminal funds transformed into a clean funds.

If money laundering would be a company, it would probably be the 4th largest company in the world.

Unfortunately, in Sicily money laundering is very common as Malta is very close, just next door.

An economic crisis could damage a business. Owners and entrepreneurs will do anything to save a business from bankruptcy. This is where the Mafia would ask an everyday favour to an everyday business such as a coffee shop, street food, barber shop, clubs and casinos to clean dirty cash with bank transactions between different accounts.

It is difficult to get evidence because if you have the right connections and you don't have a criminal record, you look like a genuine person that would be a good source of money.

That feeling is amazing.

Especially when you have such huge amounts of cash around you.

The first time that I had the opportunity to see all that cash, I asked my friend to take a photo of me wearing my bikini; my body was covered with thousands of banknotes.

My body was worth a fortune!

But what do we really know about money laundering?

Money laundering made its first appearance following the 1988 Vienna Convention and shortly thereafter became the focus of the Financial Action Task Force (FATF), established in 1989 to put in place the international anti-money laundering (AML) policy.

The evolution of money laundering legislation and regulation over the last 30 years is depicted in the AML.

This provides a very clear visual representation of the dramatic escalation of legislative and regulatory measures, from the 1988 Convention through to a series of FATF Recommendations (Recommendations), themselves prompting the enactment of European directives, national regulations, and laws.

As illustrated by the Timeline, AML policy has proven "a runaway success in terms of the extent of its diffusion', seemingly driven by the perception of an ever-expanding threat of terrorist financing and money laundering to national security and shaped by the development of the growing body of European and international guidelines and directives." Despite such extensive legislation, justification for money laundering as a separate offence has not been clearly established.

The UK economy sees trillions of pounds flow through it every single year. Inevitably some of this money is corrupt wealth – cleaned up dirty money, stolen public funds and bribes – which are given a seal of approval by passing through the UK.

According to NRA (National Risk Assessment) the best available international estimate of amounts laundered globally would be equivalent to some 2.7% of global GDP or US\$1.6 trillion in 2009.

At present, the U.K. is part of a collaborative fight against money laundering and financial crime. One of the main benefits of this is that EU member states can trace suspicious money across borders. This is achieved through access to the Europol Information System (EIS), enabling law enforcement from different countries within the EU to exchange criminal intelligence, making it much harder for criminals to cover their tracks.

So, lets write in simple terms:

How do I know if I am involved in a money laundering situation?

The most usual way that get you involved in this crime is doing a favour for a friend.

For example, a friend asks you to transfer his cash into his bank account.

Why?

You don't ask questions as you think he is your friend so you will accept it is genuine. But stop and think first about the amount of cash he is asking you to transfer into his account.

Think about where the money has come from,

Think that you will be committing a financial crime, although not aware of any bad consequences.

If the amount of this cash exceeds the £10,000 then be ready for a police interrogation.

Or maybe he says he does not have an account and asks you to pay money into your account and then transfer it to someone else. But most times, everything starts when a friend asks you to do a favour.

That favour could be also a terrorist funding.

How do you know?

Terrorist funding detection has been practiced the same way as money laundering detection ever since Counter Terrorism Funding (CTF) initiatives were added to Anti-Money Laundering (AML).

Although the two have similarities on the surface, a deeper look reveals more differences than similarities. In fact, some have rightly called terrorist funding "money laundering in reverse" because of marked differences in its sources and goals.

Do the two -warrant similar treatment in detection methods?

Or do their dissimilarities call for different detection approaches?

How are they similar?

Money laundering and terrorist financing share three similarities:

1. They involve a source of money or objects that have monetary value.

2. They involve moving the money through channels that conceal the original source.

3. This money movement and concealment of the source enables recipients to use the end funds in ways that would otherwise have exposed the initiator to legal jeopardy.

How are they different?

Admittedly, those three similarities are high-level. Their differences are at a deeper level.

Money laundering and terrorist financing usually differ in their respective source of funds. With money laundering, the initiator is an individual or organization that obtained the money through criminal activity.

This may be a single individual, as in the case of embezzlement or tax evasion.

Or it may be large criminal organizations such as The Mafia or other organised gangs operating in Russia, Eastern Europe, or America. The source, in money laundering, is always funds obtained by illicit activity.

With terrorist financing, a criminal origin is not always the case. The initial source may be legitimate. It may be wealthy benefactors who agree with terrorist goals and want to support terrorist activity. It may be groups that pose as charitable organizations, gather funds supposedly for humanitarian aid but then, either with or without the donor's knowledge, transfer the funds to terrorist groups or operatives to support their activity.

That's not to say that the source in terrorist funding is never from criminal activity. Increasingly, terrorist organizations have turned there for funding. In fact, many well-funded terrorist groups have engaged in criminal activity to eliminate reliance on donors and thus become self-supporting. Kidnappings and ransom demand by paramilitary groups, as well as trade in blood diamonds, human trafficking and arms dealing have become a growing terrorist funding source.

So, although terrorist financing might use criminal activity as a funding source, the difference between money laundering and terrorist financing is this:

In money laundering, the source of funds is always criminal activity; in terrorist financing, funding sources may be either legitimate or illicit.

Money laundering and terrorist financing differ also in the typical size of monetary transactions involved and the methods used to move them. In money laundering, the amount of funds is generally large. This requires initiators to be both more careful and more creative in the ways they move funds.

Most often, they start by breaking funds into smaller amounts to avoid triggering immediate alerts tied to size of deposits. Then they place those smaller amounts into financial institutions as multiple deposits in multiple accounts under multiple names, to make the placement of funds look as natural as possible.

Therefore, it is so important to be very careful when your trustworthy friend gives you some cash asking you to move a quantity of money from your account into another one.

Refuse the favour or find out why he is asking.

After breaking funds into small quantity, they transfer that money, bit by bit, into other financial institutions – often in countries whose banking laws allow greater anonymity and, from there, into yet other institutions.

As previous mention, Malta and Switzerland are the most popular for that. Banking covers in Africa and China are also great places for criminals to operate from.

By continually moving the money through multiple institutions, they seek to create layer upon layer of transfers until the paper trail is too complex to trace back to its original source.

Along the way, they may use informal financial systems that protect sender's and recipient's identities, such as the Middle Eastern hawala, Chinese fei chi'en or South American Black-Market Peso Exchange.

They may also send the money through shell companies that exist to create false invoices that give the impression that money was received for real goods or services, thus making it look legitimate.

Eventually, though, the money is reintegrated back into financial institutions under the real names of the initiators, but now with a string of transactions that give the illusion of being revenues from legitimate businesses.

At this point, the initiators can use the money as legitimate wealth, because the trail back to its illicit source has been obscured beyond the ability of law enforcement to trace.

Contrast that to terrorist financing, where the amount of funds generally is smaller.

These smaller amounts – and the original legitimacy of the funds – require less creativity to move without triggering alerts. In fact, one of the greatest challenges in detecting terrorist funding transactions is that they so closely mimic legitimate money movement.

This makes it easier to use financial institutions – either at the beginning of the process, at the end or all the way through.

That does not mean that financial institutions are the only means used.

Couriers sometimes smuggle cash from country to country, to move it into countries that have more relaxed detection systems.

But, again, traditional financial systems are heavily used because of their ability to move money vast distances at the push of a computer key.

So, both money laundering and terrorist funding rely heavily on the lightning-quick ability of financial institutions to move cash. This is important to remember as we continue looking at the similarities and differences of the two processes.

When we look at the intended destination and purpose of funds, money laundering and terrorist financing are completely different.

In money laundering, funds come full circle back into the criminals whose illicit activities created them. The goal is long-term: to disguise criminally obtained funds so they build a seemingly legitimate accumulation of personal wealth for their criminal perpetrators while keeping the criminal activity that generated them secret.

With terrorist financing, on the other hand, funds move from the hands of donors who usually obtained them legitimately, into the hands of criminals who intend to use them to commit illegal acts. The goal is short-term: to pay terrorist operators to commit highly public criminal acts (terrorist attacks) while concealing the originator's connection to those acts.

So, the destination and purpose of funds is dramatically different. Money laundering starts with perpetrators of criminal acts and returns all funds to those same perpetrators, only now looking legitimate and keeping the perpetrators' past criminal activity secret.

Terrorist financing pays others to commit crimes that receive maximum publicity yet keep the donors' involvement secret.

How can money laundering and terrorist financing be discovered?

For all their differences, both rely on financial institutions at some point in their transfer process. This creates a vulnerability that can enable detection.

In many ways, detection methods for both are similar.

In both processes, following recommended Counter Terrorism Funding (CTF) and

Anti–Money Laundering (AML). practices enable detection. Know Your Customer (KYC) and Customer Due Diligence (CDD) practices require specialized units in financial institutions to perform thorough verifications of prospective customer identities and backgrounds before the institution accepts them as customers.

Units dig deeper into customer applications to determine whether the customer is the account's beneficial owner or only a representative.

If so, the units must investigate the beneficial owner as well as the representative.

KYC/CDD units also compare prospective customers, representatives and beneficial owners against money laundering and terrorist watch lists to whether determine they – or any individuals with whom they have connections – are on those lists.

Only after going through this exhaustive screening process can the institution accept the prospective customer.

The initial investigation is not the end of the KYC/CDD unit's work, though. It also involves understanding the typical banking activities the institution can expect of each customer and continuously monitoring for possible signs of money laundering activity or terrorist financing involvement.

Monitoring doesn't stop with the institution's customers, either. It also involves assessing the reputation of institutions to or from which customers send or receive transfers. It involves flagging customers who maintain relationships with questionable institutions or engage in transactions with countries considered lax in their detection efforts.

And it involves applying counter-terrorist intelligence provided by government agencies to further inform assessments of customers and related institutions.

The differences between money laundering and terrorist financing are striking in origination, scope, use and purpose. Yet their joint reliance on using the infrastructure of financial institutions offers opportunities for detection.

Even terrorist financing, with its additional challenges of smaller transaction amounts and initial legitimacy of most funds, can be detected by a dedicated detection team.

 The key is for the institution to actively practice strong KYC/CDD procedures in all aspects of opening accounts, monitoring activity for suspicious behaviour, and assessing the legitimacy of funds transferring both into and out of those accounts.

These practices offer the best chance for an institution to detect and avoid attempts to use it as a vehicle for money laundering or terrorist funding.

Corruption is unfortunately both the key and the heart of money laundering.

Couriers could be identified as well but not under different circumstances such as for example an Ambulance driver.

You would not suspect that an Ambulance on duty working with emergencies cases, might be one of the links in the chain of a financial crime.

An old lady as well could look genuine on people eyes, same as a child or teenager. Even a baby's pram.

How could this happen? Easy:

An ambulance driver would transport say 100.000,00 euros in cash, all dirty money from criminal activities. He stops at the border; any border where he will meet an ordinary looking lady in her sixties; the lady then takes all the cash from the driver.

She would be travelling to say Dubai, investing all the cash in gold, getting official receipts.

The movement of funds has been accomplished. The dirty money is now clean, but made to look as unsuspicious as possible, she would then break that gold, investing the funds into small financial goods, property and a variety of investments.

The dirty money is integrated now, clean, and almost impossible trace back to the first source of the criminal activities or the ambulance driver.

The only way how to stop such financial crime is to identify the criminal activities and detect the source of the transactions, stopping corruption.

Increase the check points. Check points for everyone.

If every individual would be strong enough to refuse illegal activities in exchange of money, this could be a first step to stop money laundering.

If everyone would follow the ethical codes, with morality and honesty, that would avoid corruption, doing the right thing will save us all from frauds and financial crimes.

Dad back in town, fight or forgive?

After eight years of a fantastic close relationship with Elvis, my single life was very different:

The bed is huge, the shower always clean, the house looks very organized all the time, the smell is fresh like when you buy flowers on the first day and they smell good.

The guy next door has noticed that I was returning home alone every night.

He invited me for dinner, but I was not in a mood to be around people. Friends were coming back into my life and after six months my life is back to normal, I still think about Elvis but not like before; in a positive way this time. To stay strong, I keep following my routine and healthy lifestyle. So, I have decided to keep my mind busy, join a boxing class, study business, play tennis during the week-end and have dinner with friends and nights out as well in the club. I had a contract with FBI in Sicily for about one year. When I saw Sicily on my mission program, I went to my officer and asked why?

He only said:

— Never escape from the problems!

Identify it, resolve it, forget it!

Sicily is your place Vanessa; you should be happy to be there near your family!

Officer, Can I maybe go to Kosovo or Iraq instead? I smiled and try to convince him.

There was nothing I could do to change his mind.

Therefore, with some camomile tea and few glasses of wine I decided to sign that contract.

A week later, I flew from Germany to Rome, then from Rome to Catania.

My Mum was at the airport with flowers and my Grandparents were waiting for me in the house to have a family lunch.

I started to get all those old memories back, those I could not erase from my mind; that smell of the Mediterranean Sea reminding me of when I was little, with that scooter, with Laura and my friends, then the negative memories came to my mind like lightning striking.

Is difficult to be in the place that you hate the most and you love the most; it is like an interminable unwinnable battle with yourself. One to one with yourself.

That afternoon,

I called Laura and told her that I was in Sicily for about one year.

I met her in that afternoon.

Since I left, I kept Laura's details and used different mobile phones to contact her, just for safety reasons; I did the same with my family.

On my bed, there are a lot of letters:

Then I hear my mother's voice:

Vany! Those letters are for you love; I didn't open it as there is your name on it!

Thanks Mum I say.

My luggage is wating to be unpacked, but I am curious to open those letters first.

Bills, Advertisements, and bank statements.

Suddenly I noticed that I received a few letters from Prison.

Giuseppe had written me a letter:

And written recently as well, what a surprise!

I saw these words on that white paper saying:

Dear Vanessa,

I am sorry about everything, I asked you too many things to do for me, I didn't understand when I was hurting you because I was too busy with things.

You never refused to help me, with your smile, your energy, your love.

I miss your positivity; I will pay a fortune just to see you once again.

I am here as you know, they Judge gave me twenty years, I don't know if I can stay here without you, I would rather die. I need you. Please if you see this letter, come to visit me.

Love,

Giuseppe

For a moment I had a sensation of being stabbed in the back.

I didn't know that he was in Prison, that was a shock to me.

Then a second letter from prison:

Dear Vanessa,

We have done a lot of things together,

I am writing to thank you for everything you did for me, anytime you stay quiet and defend me. I never forgot your kindness and your smile.

I am here again this time for about 10 years

Stay safe,

Mario

Well, Mario was my boyfriend, when we were selling firearms; he was with me at that time, trying to save his back many times as he used to put the gun on the top of the car then drive off without it. Several times I said to the big boss that was my fault as I was tired because of the School hours.

Wow this is a cold shower,

Laura was right about the end of this circle.

I took a break from those letters, then went to the kitchen and spent time with my Pet and my Mum.

The doorbell rang

Hello? Who is this? I say

Vany! It is me, Laura!

Laura? She walked in with a child....

Vanessa! Oh my God It has been such a long time...she hugs me tight; you are so beautiful she added.

Well, I did say I have a surprise for you!

She points her finger to the babe. This is the surprise, she said.

Matteo? Say Hi to Aunty Vanessa

Matteo, you look so cute, how old are you? I say

I am five years old! Wow, you are a Superman now! I added.

Laura told me about Matteo's father,

He was a bad guy, a loser, an alcoholic, and she was divorcing him.

Vanessa, it is ok, that happens, that's life she says.

I am not here only for that…. There is something that you need to know:

It is about your father, she added.

My father?

Yes, Vanessa, your Dad is back in the city. I saw him once at the shop with sunglasses and a hat on his head; he looked like he doesn't want to be discovered, he is hiding something and you will be the best person to find out now.

You can use your FBI ID to follow him or maybe you just watch outside his door….

My legs are shaking again, it has been a long time since that happened.

I pause, I think,

Well Laura, I have a life now and I am out of it, I don't want to go back in that game.

She insists Vanessa, it is your Dad, he is still your Dad, you should see him and meet him!

I know it is hard, as he left you in 2003, but now you are a strong independent woman, no longer his young girl, and you would just meet him for a coffee nothing more. I think he will be very happy to see you.

Mum? Mum?

Yes, Love.

Mum, did you know that Dad is back here again?

Yes, honey I knew that, I did not say anything as I didn't want to upset you.

I was feeling very nervous as everyone knew that my father was back in the city...and nobody called to tell me about it. Crazy!

I found out where he lives. Then I decided to be the 'man' of the situation, considering the fact that he was maybe scared to be discovered by the family, that he was back in town.

I was driving an Alfa Romeo Mito at that time, black and manual. I did enjoy the feeling of smoking a cigarette and playing a good tunes while being connected with its speed. I turned off the car and waited in the parking zone, as according to Laura, my Dad was there.

His car was parked there. . I sat in my car, read a book, had a latté, and then a few hours later he was there.

He was ready to walk towards the front door with his keys. He had the same look as when he left that day. Now after 13 years, I still remember that time, yes that day, just like a cd winds back to the start , that memory can never be replaced or erased from your mind. It is permanent.

The emotion is huge, too difficult to stay calm. My first thought is to get out of my car, then slap his face and push him in the floor, telling him how much he had hurt me during these many years. But then my Angel is calling me to pull me in the opposite direction, my instinct telling me that he is still my father and that contact and explanation can bring forgiveness which can heal all my scars and turn that damage into a positive experience.

My mind was fighting, two personalities inside me, one is anger and madness, the other is peace and forgiveness.

114

How can I find the balance?

I saw him shaking hands with another guy then he walked into the flat.

I stalked the other guy to see what he was doing.   He went to a pharmacy, then, suddenly, he was waiting from someone. I waited too.

A familiar looking guy approached him.   Who could that other guy be?   I tried to remember, thinking back through my past life, yes, I know that guy, he is Giuseppe's Brother. Is that a coincidence or is something bad going on?

If my father was kidnapped, ran away, or disappeared for so long, it was always because of Giuseppe and his Boys; so why now are they connecting with my Dad?

It is something that I don't really understand.

I didn't want to go to that guy and talk with him, so I prefer to wait to hear every word that my Dad has to say.

It is late evening, I stopped by at my uncle's shop, then said:

Hi! From the car window.

He saw me, he began looking me into my eyes.

Vanessa? Oh my God! You are so pretty! Where have you been, it has been such a long time! Would you like a coffee? He added, with his fake smile.

I never forget my Dad's family. The were so attached to money and the business, without considering my mother who was left alone and had to raise me by herself; they never ever tried to give any help to support my mum, morally or financially.   They were so cold in their hearts, those kind of rich people with the envy for a sincere person like my mum.

They were aware of my Dad's departure. I didn't know, I was not aware about anything; the only thing they did during all these dramatic years was forced me to sign for every note I used to receive from them. Then, taking a photo of me with those notes in my hands as an evidence that I was satisfied with their money. I was too young to understand what was in their minds.

Now everything is coming back to me, natural, real, as a confirmation that what I supposed was not wrong. These people are not my family, I hope that their blood is not shared in my body, because I never met such stingy people in my life.

That kind of person who prefers money instead of helping a child, giving every excuse just for running the business, the more money they earned, the more they wanted.

My Grandmother used to give me money in the cradle, under the mattress, I was about two years old.   My mum she was disappointed, as she was also praying while placing that money, as if she was practicing some superstitious way to make me addicted to materialism.

I drunk that coffee than asked about my Dad.

So, Is Dad in town?

 I heard. Where does he live?

I knew where he was living, I just asked that question to see what my Uncle would tell me.

Yes, Vanessa, he is around, he is living in your Uncle's Flat, the one opposite the Piazza.

Of course, I know where he was.

Cool, May I have his number please so I will able to call him?

Sure, Vanessa, but is maybe better if I ask him first?

You really want to ask my Father, if he allows you to give his number to his own Daughter?

You seem cold Uncle, is everything all right with you? I added.

It is not that, Vanessa, I really do care about you, I just do not want to be in the middle of anything! He says.

I really feel there is something bad now, and try to control my emotions…. then I said :

Hey Uncle, Don't Worry, I will not put you in the middle of anything, you are not going to be involved, I can guarantee this to you, now please can I have that number?

As soon I get what I want, I gave a cold hug, then walk to my car.

Finally, I can get in touch with the man who has damaged my life and have a meeting face to face.

I took the elevator, press level number four, reach my flat, hiding that piece of paper with a number in my jeans packet as though it was my first date.

I spoke with my Mum,

she thought the best idea will be to meet him with a lawyer or a guard because after all these years nobody know what his intentions are…

I didn't want to put my Lawyer in the middle of this, I just want to have a one to one with Dad, therefore, I summoned up some courage and dialled his number….

The phone rang.

Hello? Who is this?

Dad? Its me?

My heart stopped for a moment, in one moment nothing was going through my mind.

His voice sounded scared.

Vani! My love, where are you?

I am in Town! Can we meet?

I have a car I can pick you up.

Yes! Come by the Piazza I will get ready and wait for you there.

I decided to wear a dress and put make up to make sure I will look as best as possible.

So, He will regret all these years he left me....

I want to make sure that he understands what he missed looking at every part of my outfit!

I am driving towards that Piazza; I parked the car then got out and saw him walking.

After all these years the word Dad could not come to my mouth very easily.

Hi D...Da...Dad, sorry Dad is just been long time that I am not saying this word, cannot really saying...How are you? How you been?

He tried to hug me, I was shaking and so much emotion in my body that I forget what I supposed to ask.... Like when you study so hard for that subject then you are there on front your teacher forgetting the words and the subject to say.

Like a singer that is trying to sing every day in his house as soon he steps on to the stage , he gets shy and stops.... I was stuck in that space and time.

I talk to myself, come on Vanessa, you can do this. Then the light returns and my voice is back.

Dad you hurt me, you make me a piece of shit, you destroyed my life, you left me without saying a word, that day at the School, I was in the hospital when I crashed the scooter, Where were you?

Where were you when I had my first boyfriend, when I had my 18th Birthday Party, my communion in the church, you missed everything Dad.

You missed 13 years of my Life. I preferred to think you were dead instead of disappearing like a ghost, where are your balls?

I was looking for you everywhere, you left Mum by herself without money and support.

Dad really? I thought you were clever!

Dad, you made me to be aggressive so that I could not trust anyone and could not open my heart anymore. You missed a lot, and trust me that time can never come back, Every Christmas I used to pray to God for your return, asking Santa Claus to give me a Dad instead of a present!

Really Dad? You made my pay your council tax for about ten years, and the bills and the debts you had with people around the town.

You owe me more than fourteen thousand euros that I wasted on your debts.

I could pay for my Master's with that money!

Do you really understand what this means?

I stop my negative talking to him then I pause taking a break, I was sitting in a public area by the Piazza and I try to listen him as well.

He was very quiet then He says:

Vani! You said you was damaged, you were hurt, you had scars in your body.

You look fine, I don't see any of those bloody scars that you have mentioned!

Suddenly, I thought about my mother, those words she mentioned about my dad's mental health.

This guy was not my father anymore!

He was acting as a wolf, maybe because he was to much time by himself or because he was isolated and couldn't reach home as he wanted but doesn't matter because a Father should do anything for his child.

He was happy to see me of course but I didn't expect that words he said.

I thought he was there to hug me and get our relationship back. I was ready to forgive him.

I decided to give him another chance,

I was stupid, I did not realize that my Dad was not acting as a father anymore.

What is his role now? What mask is he wearing now?

Why is he cold to me?

Why is he meeting with a friend, and why he does he get in touch with Giuseppe's Brother?

I feel those knives stabbing me in the back again. He is not going to help me with my scars because that guy was just a guy even if I was born from his sperm but that was not my blood anymore that guy was another person.

I was thinking to spend more time with him and try to understand until I saw a letter on my house door from a Legal adviser saying:

Dear Ms Nocera,

I am writing to you to suggest you selling the house

According to a financial investigation

You live a comfortable life, drive an expensive car, have a good career,

It would be appropriate to put your home on the market as your father owns a 50% share of this property. I strongly advise this as he is struggling with money and could potentially be under a financial depression soon. Selling the property will benefit your father's income and personal life.

I look forward to hearing from you.

Your sincerely

Legal Team

I was shaking my hands when I saw that letter!

Cannot believe really who that guy was anymore, a Devil, an enemy, wherever he was, everything he will touch or interact will be broken and demolished immediately.

I was so emotional that I decided to contact him.

Phone is ringing:

Hello? He answers

Hi, Dad or whichever entity is on your body,

Why did you send the legal letter?

I thought you would be happy to continue our relationship.

I don't know who you are anymore.

Vany I am sorry I cannot talk!

Please call the Lawyer if you want to get in touch with me!

Have a good day! He hung up.

Idiot! I am an Idiot, but I cannot regret anything because he was crazy for sure and mad but I was ready to forgive him, which means, I had that energy to forget about all the problems that he gave me. I also spoke with a police officer about him.

Giuseppe was involved in my Dad's kidnap.

But my father was not kidnapped, he escaped from Giuseppe.

Apparently, they used to work together before, then when Euro caused the financial crisis, they decided to open a business together and my father did not recognize his share in the business, although he was giving him more than the 50% of the capital.

My father apparently made me do all those things because he knew I was the only person that still believed in him, that's why when I had those phone calls he never mentioned where he was, he was telling me that he was coming soon , but he never did.

The police officer confirmed that he saw my father in town after Giuseppe was arrested.

Because if Giuseppe knew that my father was in town, he will do something bad to him.

Giuseppe hated my father, he never told me that.

My Father was in contact with Giuseppe's Brother because he was asking more money for that business, pretending to be victim of a failure, that doesn't exist anymore as he never paid for anything and closed down the business when he left.

My father was ruined, so he decided to run away with Giuseppe's money.

Now he is desperate, with no money, the only solution will be selling the house where my mother and I are living but although I was tempted I would never do such a cold thing to my mother. The share was half on my name so I had the power to get back to his Lawyer with a legal adviser that confirm, I was paying all his bills and I never received any financial support from him.

I was in the middle of a battle between Giuseppe a criminal boss and My Father a total liar .

I thought my Father was kidnapped.

He was never kidnapped.

Everything was planned by the two of them, so nobody could understand what was going on.

Giuseppe used me, against my father making me do all those bad things just because I was his daughter.

My dad was the one who mentioned my name to Giuseppe telling him that can help him out with those things!

According with my Lawyer and the investigation team, my father was in debt for over two million euros.

Giuseppe tried to help him, but he asked to have his name in the business and he refused.

My father asked him for more money for that name, but as soon as my father got his money, he ran off , my uncle closed that business a month later due a fake economic crisis.

Who was the Criminal then?

My father or Giuseppe?

I have decided to go to my Father's house for the last time.

I rang his doorbell:

Trying to be nice! I was acting very fake.

I had my plan.

I was outside his house, nobody seems to be there.

Dad, Can I come in? I need to talk with you!

I want to get back our relationship, please let me in!

Suddenly a noise,

He opened the door, I went upstairs, I saw his face.

I pushed him against the wall. I took a chair and hit it over his head, then pushed him again against the wall .

Blame him, it is everything he did to me over these 13 years.

He is not alone in the house.

I heard a baby crying.

Two young boys are saying to me:

Stop! Please! Leave daddy alone! Don't hurt Daddy please!

Those voices stopped me from a murder.

I had two brothers, he never told me that I had siblings.

I don't care anymore. I walked away from the flat left him on the floor, alive.

I won the other 50% of the property after six months legal battle.

I was in the Court and the Judge gave me 100% of the rights, therefore I won the case.

My father is happy with another family now.

I am happy to be without a Father in my life, my brothers need more support than I do. , Unfortunately his negative energy is a strong influence in my life, and I need to protect my own mental health.

Everyone has his right to choose what they prefer in their life.

Unfortunately, you cannot choose your Parents.

But you can choose your happiness, therefore as soon my contract was nearly ended , I decided to visit him and meet my brothers.

I told him, that although all the arguments we had in the past, I was ready to forgive him.

Which is what I did, not because he deserved it but because it was the right thing to do, to keep myself clear and honest; I didn't want to live a guilty life.

He shook my hand saying:

See you soon!

See you soon Dad!

See you soon is better than a Goodbye!

I walked away that I was feeling stronger than ever not because I was winning against my father but because my actions, made the difference between me and my father...

Her 30's shades of grey

Being the most respected girl in the neighbourhood is a great feeling. When I walked into a bar, someone would always welcome me with a warm smile, ready to offer a drink and something to eat. When I went to the Supermarket, the owners gave me extra items free of charge. At school, I would get free books for the year. I never paid the monthly fee for using the gym either and I never paid the entrance to get into a club. Friends used to call me every day and they invited me for baking cakes or cookies in their house, to go horse riding and many other activities. My life was very rewarding at that time! But I wasn't showing myself, I was wearing a mask. Why? Because that mask was helping me to be respected. Behind that theatre full of actress, dancers, and artists you will find the real me, once those theatre's curtains close, the real person is there. My dark side, that side was a mystery side, hard to discover, hard to recover, hard to change. I did hurt many people because I was not ready for the change, to let that part go away was too hard, or maybe I was too good in wearing that mask that they couldn't see my real personality.

I didn't believe in the love, as the trauma was given to me by my Dad was too hard to ever trust another man. I never saw myself settling down with a guy; it was impossible to have that picture in my mind.

Therefore, anytime I was having sex, it was as if biological exercise for me. I never slept with a guy after a one-night stand. I used to smoke a cigarette with them, that was the only time that I gave to a man after having sex, 3, maybe 4 minutes until I was finishing that cigarette, then get ready and walk away. Don't look back.

I did try to enjoy sex, but my fantasies were far from what I thought for normal couples.

I discovered orgasms when I was young, too young. I used to play with myself when my school mates used to play with their dolls.

One day, I was alone at home. My friends came over to do some homework for a school project. We decided to watch the Titanic, but inside the VHS machine, there was a porn movie.

I was feeling guilty because when I looked into their inno-cent eyes, I saw true purity. For about a month, they thanked me so much for that day, as they never talked about sex with their parents and they never mentioned how it worked or all those forbidden mysteries related to that subject.

I used to buy a pack of condom and show them how to use it in case they wanted to lose their virginity and did not want unwanted surprises.

I lost my virginity when I was 14 years old.

The lucky guy came to my high school; not to take classes, but to sell weed.

One day, I was looking into his eyes and he smiled at me. Then he turned on the scooter and rode towards me and said,

Hi, I am Tony.

He stood with his hand on front me and I stopped, gazing at him, loosing myself into those brown eyes, I return the hand shaking then asking him why he was having a scar in his hand...

This scar was my pet, he responded.

Hard to believe, it was looking more as a knife scar.

I am Vanessa, by the way I said.

Are you looking for some weeds? I have some cocaine.

Try some, is free for you, you will love it, he added.

Tony, thanks for your offer, I don't smoke weeds, I don't use Cocaine and I don't drink either.

I had never been attracted to drugs. However, I used to drink some wine with my family; my grandfather has a vineyard that produces wine grapes. I used to drink one glass of that wine at lunch time every Sunday and feel very sleepy afterwards.

I gazed at him, then said:

I just think you can do better than that,

you should study! I added.

He looks at me up and down with his eyes, being quiet, then he left,

A short while later, on a summer day, I was walking home from school.

I heard someone called my name...

Vanessa! Vanessa!!!

Then a noise of the scooter, ridden by Tony.

Hi Tony, good to see you, what are you up to? I said

Fancy of a ride around the costs? He said

I checked the time, then I say...

Only if you could take me home in one hour!

Tick! He assured me

The air is fresh, my hair is across my face from the helmet. Just us two on the scooter surrounded by the landscape of the Mediterranean Sea. He took my hand and placed it on his belly, my legs are shaking, butterflies in my stomach. I can feel the smell of salt in my nostrils, giving me a sensation of freshness, all the while he is holding my hand so tight. I feel his chest, then he stops the scooter in the middle of the street telling me...

I forget something....

Tenderly, he placed his hands over my cheeks then kissed me for about 30 seconds.

I cannot remember the exact time, but I remember it was a long never-ending kiss.

That day was the first of our many days together.

Tony was my first Boyfriend. He was tall and his skin colour was quite dark, with black hair and flat brown eyes. He had a beauty spot, on his right cheek, that was looking good on his face, was a bit sexy. He would wear a denim jacket and timberland shoes; he had a tattoo on his neck, going up to his left ear.

Whenever I planned a date with Tony, I had to lie to my Mum and hide from friends because they would not approve. He had a bad reputation around the city; a twenty-one-year-old boy with 4 years behind the bars, but with me he was the sweetest guy.

It is a bank holiday weekend and mum is working. I went to his house and immediately he made me feel comfortable. He ran a bath for me. He lit candles and handed me a glass of wine. Then he began to wash my back, again and again with the sponge, crossing his legs over my legs. He licked my breast and touch it with the sponge; then touching me all over my body then with his overwhelming eyes he said

Would you like to make love with me?

I think for about few seconds,

Yes! I said.

He took a towel, putting it over my back then kissing my shoulder and say

I am waiting for you in the bedroom.

Unfortunately, it was not good as I expected or hoped in my dreams and fantasies.

It was my decision to stay with Tony in his house; I took a risk to see what he was really like.

Where this could lead.

That wasn't love as I was expected.

He started to remove my towel, waiting until I was laying on bed.

I was feeling different, my arms are waving in the air and my vision is blurred.

While I am still very dizzy I am looking at him telling him that I am not well but he continued kissing me, saying

Relax, Is just you and I here,

Don't think about anything

The room is spinning around me.

In the meantime, he took a rope and started to tie my ankles next to furniture, then he handcuffed me over the back of his bed.

I knew then he had drugged me.

He had added ecstasy in my drink; the last thing that I remember was his look when he took off his boxer shorts.

When I woke up, I found blood over his bedsheet, my blood. He had gone.

I got dressed and ran away from that monster...

I had been raped. I lost my virginity to a monster.

In my sweet innocence, I had considered that guy to be a perfect gentleman, but I was wrong. Boy was I wrong!

A few months later, I saw a newspaper with his picture in it, saying that he was arrested as they have found heroin and morphine in his house.

I was happy about that because I then had my revenge.

I never said a word to my friends about him or to my Mum as nobody was aware that I was seeing such a horrible person.

With that bad experience behind me, I started dating regular guys of course.

I did have a lovely Boyfriend who treated me very well; he never let me down, but I just had my shades, my need, and live with it and it was not my fault.

When you have had a traumatic experience, if this is not carefully treated taking time with love, attentions, or therapy, it can affect the entire future leading into sadness and negativity for the rest of your life.

I was running away from serious relationship and I guess that made me hurt most of my boyfriends for being selfish and hard to be loved.

I used most of them to satisfy my own fantasies, then throw them away like objects, binned like scrap paper, items that have served their purpose, my purpose. Use them instead of being used by them.

As soon I was satiated, I did not care too much about them. My sexual pleasure was made from, and now resided in, tortures.

Cuddling, kissing, massages, watching romantic movies, gentle sex, I did not like all of that.

After the trauma with Tony, I was dating a lovely guy when I told about him, he was trying to make me very comfortable with my sexual life.

After that, I found myself again. As my pleasure, I added the addiction of adrenaline, it was like you drive a motor-bike and you go really fast, although you know is danger-ous, that speed gave me a feeling of freedom, energy and relaxation as well, of being fully alive. It is hard to believe that I fell asleep going at that speed, especially when my partner was driving and I was on the back seat, he would touch 220Km/ph.

He thought I would be scared, not at all, as I was sleeping with that speed, in the car as well, same emotion, is hard to describe if you never try to have a situation that you like and you enjoy but on the other hand, you crazily risk your life.

Sex was like this for me.

I never get tired of it especially when I was the one who took the initiative.

I didn't like to be kissed or hugged during it,

If I didn't have control of it, I didn't enjoy it so much.

My common sexual fantasy was forcing a man to satisfy my perversions.

I also had few guys who lost their virginity with me.

One of them was hurting to much with me that he was crying about it, I did not care while he was hurting, as he agreed to have extreme sex with me.

When I want to have some fun, I used to take the guy to a hotel, Or go to Laura's Garages, depending on what I had in mind. I forced them to take me from behind then, I told them to make me moan in an extreme way, if it was not painful, I did not reach the orgasm.

If the guy was to soft, I told him to leave the hotel or the house. If they saw me walking in the street, they would stop me, begging me for another chance.

I was their drug; they couldn't understand that they were victims of my shades, my deep desires.

They were addicted to me, with my perversion, and the more they stayed with me more they couldn't run away to another girl.

One meeting with me was enough for make them feel excited, happy.

It's crazy to think about it.

When you don't care, they are chasing you. People want what they can't have.

When you show them your Love, they hurt you or disappear for no reason.

Therefore, I was not engaged and when they proposed or they asked me to have a relationship, I would just thank them for the nice time, the lovely experience together, because what I really want it wasn't there or them.

I am a woman, and as you all must know by now, all women are complicated. My sexuality was complicated at same point. I also try to get with another woman, but it did not work; I didn't deserve to be loved in that way.

Maybe, I was influenced by Tony, maybe I was looking for a substitute Father, maybe I was too weak to move on and find my own happiness?

I decided to talk with a therapist about it,

She told me, to just focus on myself.

I understand that, but what part of myself?

The one that is destroyed or the one that is weak?

I could not truly express my opinion to her. She prescribed some strong sedative to make me relax and feel sleepy, but that did not fix the problem.

She was not good enough to make me face up to the Truth.

All my traumas, and all the things that my eyes had seen, stored in my mind keeping me cold and insensitive.

Is there a medicine that can make me forget about everything?

And not destroy the weak part of myself.

The only medicine was the Love.

That didn't happen overnight.

It took a lot of time, especially when you have a lot of delusion in your life, this can lead to a negative reaction.

From my life experience I strongly believe that to achieve happiness is about your reaction and the way you take that particular time.

There are different types of reaction in life; one is going to fall; one is going to improve your skills. Sink or swim. The first is usually the most common. They say, what doesn't break you, makes you stronger.

You are heartbroken for example or your family are going through a divorce.

The person with the common reaction attempts to replace that feeling with another feeling, for example to find another boyfriend or get drunk with the friends, not the true friends.

Those common friends just to have fun, going out, clubbing and leaving everything behind whiling drinking, partying and smoking, getting high and trying to wait for that time when you feel better and you will let that negativity leave you.

Many people react in different way, but they usually have the first reaction.

On the flipside there are few people, called smart people, that are clever enough to understand what kind of reaction is good to speed up that messy and uncomfortable time being a thing of the past.

Accelerate that dark side.

But How?

Knowing how to react:

You could be heart broken, your friends dumped you for another guy, someone promise to take you out for dinner during the weekend, but they never did, is your family going to divorce.

You were sacked and have a sad time, it can be any kind of negative feeling that can affect your day, your week, and your time.

This is how I have learned to control my 30 shades of grey, to ensure the light is coming first than the dark side, to protect myself against those delusions, to make sure that those delusions are going away from my mind and my heart.

If we stop and we are thinking, pause first, think about delusion, then change the word into experience and think about the positive way of it.

Learn from those delusions,

Learn from the experiences, that is the key.

If you think that those bad memories are also experiences to help you grow,

would you still be upset about them?

Because those experiences helped you understand who you really are, not how the people want you to be or what they like from you, because you are not those people, you are you.

We lost ourselves in technology facing CEOs, dealing with busy agendas, leaving our lives behind, focusing on other lives.

Stop wearing that mask and look yourself on the mirror.

Is that face familiar to you?

Is that the real you?

Or is that look hiding from that mask!

Every person is unique. But only a small percent of those people outside can really understand my words.

It is hard, I know, but not impossible.

If you are confident and you believe in yourself, it is very easy to get into the right street.

Focus!

Easy to say...

But how?

How do you believe in yourself?

Pause, think, think first about people who loved you and loving you, your family, your friends, your dog, your pet, yourself, think about you, you first, then other people, being a bit selfish is not wrong.

Believe in your skill, setting up those goals that you have, your challenges, the list of your achievement and what you really want to do next.

And think about those bad delusions and live with them every day to understand that are only experiences in your life to make you better next time, to help see that vision first, to make you the person you are now.

Because if you really think about those delusions and you crying about them, they will always be there for ever and ever, but you don't want that, you want to be successful and happy so let them go in a positive way, because if you are an adult now and conscious about living a good life, it is only because you had those experiences in your life.

You are now made of what you was before, your way to seeing thing different and take more responsibility is only because you was going on a hard section of your life when you can only be happy about, because your life was not that normal, was not that boring.

Those zigzag lines crossing your life, made your journey interesting, you should be proud of it! We all have scars of Life. I was supported by different mentors, I was loved by different guys, I was helped by different friends, teachers used to offer one to one meeting. My mother was also very important in my life. I had different therapists helping me understand that it was not my fault. It was, I think, no because I want to feel guilty. It was my fault because I could not accelerate the recovery process. If I could understand how to react at the beginning, maybe I would not waste that time sitting on the sofa eating my ice-cream. I was lazy, or maybe, I did not want to react because I feared the chance.

After that dark tunnel called Black Moon, Finally ... I saw the change! The light! The magic, the love, the sunshine, the positivity of living my life again. It wasn't about Elvis or about the love that he gave me of course that helped me out I understand how to love myself more, looking after me, conduct a healthy life, practice meditation, learning something new, being away from drugs and alcohol, not from the club as I do love dancing. You do not fall if you are an open book you fall if you keep things for yourself being isolated from the world.

My depression was caused because I never took it to serious.

I used to hide myself with the people who loved me the most. I was sick and tired of being isolated, dealing with the crime makes you grow, When you notice that you are not like them, you are better than them.

Being aware that you are different, different like the Sun and the Moon, the day, and the night.

One part of myself was fine, the other part was destroyed, but does not mean it was not there.

It was only damaged.

Is taking time to get back all those little pieces.

But once you take them and put it back, it is so rewarding.

You can finally look yourself in a different way. See the face in the mirror, your face.

You will realise, like you realise that tension that was making you feel that way, was making you feel nervous.

People are too busy to look after you and taking care of you.

But you? You can do it!

You are the only one who has that power!

Nobody can help you with that!

And if now I achieve my goals, felling happy is only because I was ready to change.

The beginning is tough, you will think ….is the right time to do it?

Is the right time to change?

You will get so many chances to implement that strength, transform your weakness into a strength into opportunity into challenges.

Because only you can benefit from that change.

Your mental health comes first.

Everyone's lives are different, and my life was very tough, hard to explain, Difficult to let it go. Going from crime to serve the Government was not easy. Two sides of your life.

The illegal and the legal together, the illicit firearm and those guns provide in the training, to help you against bad people, to protect the world.

If we can support each other more, at work, in the family, being good people, good friends, this could lead to a better world. Enjoying the simplicity of this life.

If you see something that doesn't look right, tell a friend, ask for their opinion, spread that voice, because this is the only way to stop corruption. If you face a bad person, and he/she doesn't do the right thing, And you are there, asking yourself why is he/she doing it? Don't just walk away, stop that person and make him understand why this is wrong, teaching the ethics, the morality around the world is a must for everyone on Earth.

Spread the smile, not the negativity.
Spread that Love!
Love does not cost a thing.

I thank everyone who made me the woman that I am now. Because those experiences made me strong, made me the real me. The lady that I am now.

Made me a good person but a better person....

Vanessa Nocera

She is thirty years old, a determinated lady, who sets different goals in her life. She was growing up in Syracuse, city of Sicily. Vanessa is working towards a master's degree in business, while she is also an event planner, promoting events, organizing conferences, reaching excellent targets. She is a marathon runner, raising funds to support the charity. She's over four years of military experience in the Air-force and NATO. Her ambitions will always ensure that she is successful performing in all her future undertakings. She loves travelling, learning new things, socialising and share her new projects with the workforce. Her positive attitude helps her to start a successful life in the United Kingdom.

Achievements

Thanks to my editor, Ludovico Leone, who heard this story idea and decided to help me with the editing and the publishing process. My friend Stewart who reviewed every single draft with me, encouraging me to dig deeper. Thank you to my furlough period, during the Covid-19, as this helped me to have enough time to compete with my writing. Thanks to my Mum, as during the Lockdown she was pushing me writing. A big thanks goes to you, my readers, for cheering and sharing my book.

Printed in Great Britain
by Amazon

46771862R00087